The Hidden Side of Retirement

What Nobody Tells You About Identity, Purpose, and Life After Your Career Ends

Cheryl Fimbel

For more information, contact: Cheryl@CrownYearsMedia.com

ISBN Paperback: 979-8-9948962-0-4
ISBN Electronic: 979-8-9948962-1-1

Library of Congress Control Number: 2026903992

Portions of this book are works of nonfiction. Certain names and identifying characteristics have been changed.

Printed in the United States of America.

Cheryl Fimbel
The Retirement Journey Series

CrownYearsMedia.com
Cheryl@CrownYearsMedia.com

Contents

INTRODUCTION

The Great Unknown – Navigating Your Retirement Transition

You've spent months planning two-week vacations, but you're about to enter a phase that could last 8,000 days or more. Welcome to the transition to retirement between who you were and who you're becoming.

Retiring is hard. Like, really hard. Nobody prepares you for it.

Everyone talks about the money part. Do you have enough saved? Can you afford to retire? That's important, sure. But that's not what's going to mess you up.

There's research from the Employee Benefit Research Institute - they conducted a whole study on retirement transitions - and you know what they found about the people who struggle in early retirement versus the ones who do okay? It's not about money. It's about whether they prepared for the psychological part. The practical part. All the things nobody talks about.

That's what this book is about. The things nobody warned me about. This book is the guide I desperately needed but didn't have—a day-by-day survival manual for those first 90 days after your work life ends.

When my position was unexpectedly eliminated two weeks before my 69th birthday, I decided to retire. The severance package was generous, and when our financial planner ran the numbers on my retirement accounts, she said we could make it work. So okay, I thought. We're good. We had enough money. That was the important part, right?

Wrong. Having enough money just meant I didn't have to worry about paying bills. It didn't tell me what to do with myself. It didn't fix the panic attacks at 3 AM. It didn't explain why I felt so weird about losing my work email address - like that email address mattered, but somehow it did.

And it definitely didn't help when I'd be standing in my kitchen at 10 AM on a Tuesday with no idea what I was supposed to do. There were eight hours until it was a reasonable time to go to bed.

Nobody told me about any of that.

The sudden loss of my professional identity triggered a range of emotional responses I had not expected. I quickly learned that the emotional and practical aspects of this transition were equally critical, and these lessons shaped this book.

This book gets you through the first 90 days—the survival phase. Getting your footing, not drowning.

But thriving? That's different work. That happens in months 3-24, when you move from 'I got through today' to 'I'm building something that actually matters to me.

That's why I'm continuing this journey with you in the companion book, which picks up where this book leaves off and addresses the deeper work of building sustainable systems, finding purpose, and creating a retirement that genuinely fulfills you. But first, let's get you through these crucial first 90 days.

Turn the page and begin preparing for your transition—not just financially, but emotionally and practically. Your future self will thank you for the intentionality you bring to this crucial passage.

Let's begin by exploring the most fundamental question: How do you know when you're truly ready to retire.

CHAPTER 1

How to Know You're Ready
(and Stop Second Guessing Yourself)

"Retirement is the only time in your life
when time no longer equals money."
— Unknown

The journey to retirement readiness begins long before you leave your office for the last time. For some, it's a carefully planned transition. For others, like me, it arrives unexpectedly. Either way, understanding what actual readiness means—financially, emotionally, and practically—can make all the difference.

My own journey began five years ago when I started seriously considering retirement. I wanted to wait until I was at least 70 to receive the full Social Security benefits. But two weeks after we buried my mother, I got the phone call that changed everything. I'd been laid off. At two weeks before my 69th birthday, I wasn't ready—I wanted to work one more year. But ready or not, retirement had chosen me.

It shouldn't have been as big a surprise as it was. Last year, my boss told me they were reviewing our department and reevaluating everyone's position. My boss said nothing would likely happen before the end of the year, but a decision would be made in the first quarter. I was so preoccupied with my mother's failing health that I wasn't thinking about it during that time.

April 14th. I'll never forget that date. My boss called me. Thirty seconds into the conversation, my 45-year career was over.

I don't even know what I felt at first. Numb, I think. Then upset. Then numb again. They kept telling me it wasn't personal. The position was being eliminated. Restructuring. All the corporate language.

But it was my position. My desk. My job for 8 years and my career of 45 years. How is that not personal?

The sixteen-week severance was generous; I'll give them that. I sat with our financial planner the next week, scared to ask the fundamental question: Can we afford for me never to work again? She ran the numbers and said yes, we could do this. We may not be able to travel often or make large expenditures, but we will be fine. I had such a sense of relief, but it was mixed with anxiety. The money would work. But I had no clue if I would.

Here's what I learned through this unexpected transition: you absolutely need enough money - without it, no amount of positive thinking will fix the stress of wondering if you can pay your bills. But most retirement books won't tell you that money alone doesn't make you happy in retirement. You know what I see happening? Someone has their finances nailed down - the 401(k) is solid, the budget's set - and then they hit retirement and fall apart. Why? Because they never once thought about who they'd be without that job title.

Those empty Tuesday mornings? They never planned for those. The loneliness when the work friends... disappear? Never saw it coming. Financial security gets you through the door, sure. But then what? It doesn't tell you what to do with yourself once you're standing there.

The solution is a comprehensive approach that builds on your financial foundation with a practical 90-day psychological and lifestyle roadmap—precisely what this book provides. Think of it this way: your finances get you to retirement's door, but emotional and practical preparation determines whether you'll thrive once you walk through it.

My experience taught me that retirement readiness has multiple dimensions, and I was only prepared for one of them. Looking back, I realize I'd failed almost every test that mattered. I was "Cheryl the Director" with no idea who plain "Cheryl" was. People I spoke with daily were work friends. My husband Ed and I had never seriously discussed what 24/7 togetherness would mean for us. If you want to assess your own readiness across all these dimensions—not just financial—turn to the **Retirement Readiness Assessment Suite** in Toolkit #1 at the end of this chapter. These are the assessments I wish I'd had.

The Hidden Factors Most People Overlook

There are many books available that list activities like visiting museums or trying new things, but they often lack deeper insight into readiness. I want to address not just the money, but also the hidden readiness factors that most people overlook.

When you're still working but thinking about retirement, at least you have something to look forward to. But once you're actually there? You'd better have thought through what comes next, or you're in trouble.

I see people who retire and then spend their days just watching TV. It breaks my heart. They worked for decades, built careers, contributed so much—and now they're sitting there bored out of their minds. That's a big reason I'm writing this book. I want people to figure out what they actually want to do with all this time before they're staring at the ceiling, wondering what happened.

Here's what matters, you need to start thinking about this while you're still working. If someone asked you today what you'd do if you didn't have to go to work tomorrow, what would you say? And I don't mean vague stuff like "travel more" or "see the grandkids." I mean, actually—what would you do on a Tuesday morning? How would you fill your days?

Most of us can't answer that question. And that's precisely why retirement is so hard.

You spend decades letting work define everything. Your days, who you are, what matters. When that's gone, you're lost. I was lost.

Money isn't the only thing you need to be ready for. There are other considerations - who are you without your job? Who are you going to talk to? What's going to give you a reason to get up in the morning? How's your marriage going to handle both of you being home all day?

I've put together **The Five Pillars of Readiness** assessment in Toolkit #1 to help you think through all of that. Not just the financial part. All of it.

Why This Matters More Than Your Portfolio

Here's something that might surprise you: The American Psychological Association found that people who do the emotional homework before retiring report 42% higher satisfaction levels, regardless of their financial situation. Let me say that again—it's not the people with the most money who have the best retirements. It's the people who have prepared psychologically for the transition.

You need financial security - that's baseline. But here's what I've noticed: once you've got that covered, having even more money in the bank doesn't automatically make retirement better. What dramatically improves it is being emotionally and psychologically prepared for the identity shift, the loss of structure, the change in social connections, and the need to create new sources of purpose and meaning.

I learned this through my own experience and by talking to other retirees. The ones who struggle aren't necessarily the ones with less money; they're the ones who never thought about what their retirement would actually look like beyond just "not working."

The Research Behind My Experience

Turns out I'm not the only one who figured out that having enough money doesn't automatically make retirement work. The 2024 MassMutual Retirement Happiness Study found that emotionally prepared retirees were twice as likely to be satisfied in retirement as those who focused only on their finances.

The Stanford Center on Longevity conducted a 2023 study that really hit home for me. They found that 89% of retirees who were struggling had met their financial goals. They had enough money. But they hadn't prepared themselves psychologically for what retirement would actually be like.

That's precisely what happened to me. My bank account was ready. My head wasn't. The research confirms what I learned the hard way - if your mind and identity aren't prepared for this transition, having money in the bank won't save you from a rough time.

Getting Your Head Ready (Because Nobody Talks About This Part)

When you stop working, you don't just lose your income. The whole framework of your life ends with your job. If you think about it, for decades, work has dictated when to get up, where to go, who to talk to, and what to focus on each day. Then, suddenly, it's gone. No more coworkers stopping by your desk to chat. No more meetings to complain about (but secretly miss). No more sense that you're needed somewhere every morning.

Even if retirement feels like it's years away, don't wait to think about this. Life has a way of deciding for you. A company merger. An industry shift. A health scare. A family crisis. Any of these can push you out the door faster than you ever imagined. I got backed into a corner at 69, laid off when I thought I had one more year. You don't have to let that happen to you.

The Mistakes I Made (So You Don't Have To)

In retrospect, I can see where I went wrong, and talking to other retirees, I'm definitely not alone in making these mistakes:

Mistake #1: Thinking it's all about the money. I spent so much time worrying about whether we had enough saved that I never stopped to think about what I'd really do with myself all day. Financial security matters, but it's not the whole picture.

Mistake #2: Assuming I'd automatically love being home. I believed that retirement would mean having free time all the time— sleeping in and doing whatever I wanted without any pressure. However, I must admit that I was wrong. The first time I sat down to watch a movie at 2 p.m. on a Tuesday, I felt terrible. It was as if I were playing hooky or should be doing something instead. That guilt about "not being productive" during conventional work hours? Nobody warns you about that.

Mistake #3: Not discussing expectations with my husband. We never really talked about how things would work with both of us at home all the time. Who would manage what around the house? How much togetherness was too much? We're still working through some of that, to be honest.

Mistake #4: Waiting too long to build non-work friendships. When you've spent decades being "Cheryl the Director," it's tough to figure out who you are without that title. I wish I'd started building other parts of my identity years ago instead of letting my career be my whole world.

When Should You Start the Emotional Work?

I wish I'd thought about the emotional side of retirement years before I got laid off. Not the money part. But the questions that actually matter: Who am I if I'm not working? What's it going to be like being home with Ed all day, every day? Have I built anything outside my career that will fill these empty hours?

If you're still working and wondering when to start, the answer is now, even if retirement feels far off, especially if retirement feels far off.

Your 5-Year Retirement Preparation Journey

5+ Years Out: Start Exploring Your Identity

This is when you should begin asking yourself who you are when you're not at work. I spent decades being "Cheryl the Director" and never stopped to think about who I'd be without that title.

Start small. When you're at a neighborhood barbecue, try introducing yourself without mentioning work. Join one group that has nothing to do with your career, a book club, hiking group, or whatever interests you. Begin paying attention to what you enjoy doing on weekends that isn't catching up on work.

2-5 Years Out: Build Your Foundation

This is when the real work begins. You need to start building the life that will sustain you in retirement. I wish I'd started making friends outside of work during this period. Join something with regular meetings—not for networking, but for genuine connection.

Start stepping back from being indispensable at work. Train others to manage your responsibilities. It's hard for us "control freaks", but it's practice for letting go. Have your first serious conversations with your spouse about what retirement will really look like day to day.

1-2 Years Out: Get Specific

Now it's time to get practical. Create actual plans for your first 90 days of retirement. Start living on your retirement budget now to work out the kinks. If you haven't had those tough conversations with your spouse about household responsibilities and personal space, you can't put them off any longer.

Begin your mental transition by visualizing specific days in retirement. Not vague dreams of "travel" but actual Tuesday afternoons. What will you do when it's raining, and you have nowhere to be?

Final Year: The Emotional Work

This is when you need to start letting go emotionally, not just practically. Begin grieving the career you're leaving—yes, even if you're excited to go. Start saying your goodbyes properly. Document your legacy at work. Most importantly, start getting excited about what's next rather than just relieved that what's ending is over.

Where Are You Really?

Now that you've read the timeline, take 3 minutes to complete **The Three-Minute Gut Check** in the toolkit. Be brutally honest with yourself; nobody else needs to see your answers. These few pointed questions will tell you where you actually stand, not where you wish you were.

When You Don't Get to Choose

Some people choose when to retire. They plan it out, pick a date, and have a party. Then there are people like me. Retirement happened to me. I didn't choose it.

When you get laid off or forced out - whether it's downsizing or a health crisis or whatever - you're dealing with two things at once. The immediate shock of losing your job and trying to figure out what you're going to do with the rest of your life. Both at the same time.

I had three days. Three days to go from being Cheryl the Director to... I don't know what. Just Cheryl, I guess.

Three days to process that I'd lost the identity I'd had for 45 years. To wrap up my work. Say goodbye to people who'd become friends, not just coworkers. Turn in my laptop and my badge. Clean out my desk.

There wasn't enough time. Not even close.

And the timing? The timing was brutal. My mother's funeral was two weeks before it happened. Two weeks. I was still walking around in that fog where you forget she's gone, where the phone rings and for half a second you think it might be her.

Now I had to grieve my career too while figuring out the practical question nobody prepares you for: What exactly does a suddenly retired person do at 10 AM on a Tuesday?

When you choose your retirement date, you get to prepare emotionally, tie up loose ends, and say proper goodbyes. You get a transition period, maybe even a farewell party. I got a phone call and a severance package. The difference between choosing to leave and being told to go is the difference between a planned move and an eviction—even if you end up in the same place, how you get there matters.

You can start the mental work years in advance. The assessments and journey guide in the toolkits will help you prepare properly, whether you have five years or five weeks.

Don't Let Retirement Choose You

Here's the truth about my "retirement preparation": I didn't have a last year to get ready. I'd been mentally coasting through what I assumed would be my final year of work. For five years, I'd been doing the retirement math—checking our 401 (k) statements and running different scenarios in spreadsheets. What I wasn't doing was preparing myself emotionally for the reality of actually leaving. There was always next month, next quarter, next year to think about who Cheryl would be without the word 'Director' attached to her name. Then came that April phone call, and my 'next year' disappeared. Sixteen weeks of severance became my entire transition period from professional to... what, exactly?

I've discovered I wasn't unusual in this. We pore over our financial statements but avoid looking at the emotional landscape of retirement. We know our portfolio balance down to the penny, but can't answer what we'll do on a random Wednesday afternoon. I had different spreadsheets going - retirement income scenarios, every one of them. But a plan for how to introduce myself at a party without my job title? Didn't have that. Not even close. The irony is, once your finances are adequate—and mine were—it's the emotional and psychological preparation that determines whether those first months feel like freedom or a free fall. My spreadsheets were perfect. I was a mess.

Please don't make my mistake. I had 45 years to think about retirement, and I still screwed it up. You know why? Because I thought about the money. I ran the numbers a hundred different ways. But who would I be without my job title? What would Ed and I actually do with each other all day long? Never crossed my mind.

We'd been married for almost 48 years. You'd think we would have talked about it. But we didn't. Not really. And then suddenly I'm home, and he's home, and I don't even know whose job it is to buy groceries now. He's been doing it since he retired - so do I take that over? Does he keep doing it? Sounds stupid, right? But nobody tells you about this stuff.

Here's what I wish someone had told me: start figuring this out before you have to. Don't wait until you're retired and standing in your kitchen on a Monday morning, wondering what you're supposed to do with yourself. Build some friendships that have nothing to do with work. Find something you like doing that isn't your career. Have the awkward conversation with your spouse about what "being together all the time" actually means.

Because let me tell you, those awkward conversations? They are way less embarrassing than the argument Ed and I had on Day 53 when he came home and found I'd reorganized his entire home office.

I've been retired for eight months now. I spent most of that time messing things up and then trying to fix them.

But I figured some things out. I know now why some people are okay with retirement, and others fall apart. And it's not what retirement books talk about. It's not about money, hobbies, or bucket lists.

It's all the things nobody prepares you for. The daily realities that hit you, and you have no idea how to handle them, because nobody warned you that they were coming. That's what this book is about. The things I wish someone had told me.

If you're reading this from your office, counting down months or years until retirement, you have an advantage I didn't get: the chance to prepare while you still have the structure and identity of work to fall back on. Use that time. It's more valuable than any amount of severance.

Before you move on to Chapter 2, I strongly encourage you to complete the **Retirement Readiness Assessment Suite** that follows. Be honest with yourself; nobody else needs to see your answers. The assessments will show you exactly where you stand and what you need to work on. Then Chapter 2 will help you start building the retirement you want, not just the one that happens to you.

Toolkit #1
The Retirement Readiness Assessment Suite

This isn't about passing or failing. It's about understanding where you are and what you need to work on. Be brutally honest with yourself. Nobody else needs to see your answers.

Assessment 1: The Three-Minute Gut Check

Start here—these cut through the overthinking.

Minute 1: The Morning Question

When you wake up on Monday morning, before you even roll out of bed, what's the first feeling that comes to mind?
- Dread = Not ready yet. You're running away from work, not toward something new.
- Indifference = Getting close. Work no longer defines you, but you haven't built what's next.
- Excitement about non-work plans = Ready. You're running toward something, not away from it.

Follow-up Question: Can you name three specific things you'd do tomorrow if you didn't have to work?
- Vague answers ("relax," "travel") = not ready
- Specific answers ("finish photo albums," "volunteer at literacy center") = ready

Your three things:

____

____

____

Minute 2: The Identity Question

Complete this sentence without mentioning your job or career: "I am someone who..."

Write for 60 seconds without stopping:

____

____

____

____

____

Scoring:
- If you froze or struggled = not ready yet
- If you wrote 1-2 identities = getting there
- If 3+ identities flowed naturally = emotionally prepared

Follow-up Question: When you meet new people, could you have a ten-minute conversation without mentioning your career? Start practicing now; it's liberating to discover who you are beyond your business card.
- Yes = Ready. You've developed an identity beyond your professional role.
- No = Not ready. Your career is still your primary identity anchor.

Minute 3: The Sunday Night Question

Think about how Sunday nights feel for you right now:
- Anxious about Monday, but can't imagine not working = not ready
- Dreading Monday and fantasizing about freedom = ready or very close
- Feeling neutral = either burned out or truly ready (dig deeper)

Follow-up Question: If you won the lottery tomorrow, would you:
- Still go to work on Monday to wrap things up properly Ready. Wanting to wrap things up signals emotional closure — you're leaving on your terms.
- Call in and never return Not Ready. Wanting to bolt suggests you're escaping, not transitioning.

Your answer says a lot about whether you're emotionally complete with your career.

Your Three-Minute Score: Count your "ready" responses: ______/6 Questions

Assessment 2: The Five Pillars Of Readiness

Rate yourself honestly as "Yes" or "No" on each and count your "Yes" responses for the score:

Pillar 1: Financial Readiness
- ______ I can cover all expenses without panic
- ______ I have a buffer for unexpected costs
- ______ I understand my income sources
- ______ I'm not losing sleep over money

Score: ___/4

Pillar 2: Identity Readiness

- ______ I can introduce myself without mentioning my career
- ______ I have interests unrelated to work
- ______ My self-worth isn't tied to my job title
- ______ I know who I am beyond my professional role

Score: ___/4

Pillar 3: Social Readiness

- ______ I have friends outside of work
- ______ I belong to groups unrelated to my career
- ______ I can keep relationships without work as the connector
- ______ I've found how I'll replace workplace social interactions

Score: ___/4

Pillar 4: Purpose Readiness

- ______ I know what will make me feel useful post-retirement
- ______ I have causes or activities that matter to me
- ______ I can create meaning without external validation
- ______ I've found ways to contribute beyond paid work

Score: ___/4

Pillar 5: Relationship Readiness

- ______ My spouse/partner and I have discussed expectations
- ______ We've talked about household responsibilities
- ______ We've addressed the "24/7 togetherness" issue
- ______ We agree on retirement lifestyle and activities

Score: ___/4

Total Five Pillars Score: ___/20

If you scored less than 12, you have significant work to do before you retire. And that's okay—now you know what to work on.

The Research Behind My Experience

These five pillars aren't just something I made up. There's actual research behind them.

The Financial Planning Association conducted a 2025 survey on retirement planning trends. They found that 78% of people preparing to retire focus only on the financial aspect. But here's what matters: the people who considered all five dimensions were three times more likely to have a successful transition. Three times.

Stanford's Retirement Transition Study identified the same five factors as predictors of whether someone will be satisfied in retirement. It's not just one institution saying this - multiple studies are pointing to the same things.

The American Psychological Association conducted research on work and identity transitions. What they found was sobering. People who scored low on identity readiness - which I would have - experienced clinical-level anxiety 45% of the time during their first 90 days of retirement.

If I'd taken this assessment before I retired, it would have shown me exactly where I was vulnerable. I could have prepared for what was coming instead of getting blindsided.

Assessment 3: The Reality Check Questions

Rate yourself honestly as "Yes" or "No" on each and count your "Yes" responses for the score:

The Daily Life Test:

- _____ Can I structure an entire day without external obligations?
- _____ Do I enjoy my own company for extended periods?

- _______ Can I find fulfillment in "ordinary" Tuesday afternoons?

The Meaning Test:

- _______ Can I create purpose without a job title?
- _______ Will I feel valuable without a paycheck?
- _______ Can I handle not being "important" anymore?

The Relationship Test:

- _______ Can my marriage survive unlimited togetherness?
- _______ Do I have friends who'll stick around when I can't talk shop?
- _______ Can I make new friends without work as an icebreaker?

The Flexibility Test:

- _______ Can I manage changes in plans or things falling through?
- _______ Am I okay with days that don't go as expected?
- _______ Can I be spontaneous after decades of structure

The Health Test:

- _______ Am I retiring TO something instead of FROM something?
- _______ Is my mental health stable enough for a significant transition?
- _______ Do I have healthy ways to cope with stress and change?

Count your "Yes" answers: ____/15

Less than 10? You need more preparation. This isn't failure, it's valuable information.

Your Readiness Score Summary

Add your scores from all assessments:
Three-Minute Gut Check: ___/6
Five Pillars: ___/20
Reality Check: ___/15

Interpreting Your Results:

If you scored in the top third of each assessment:
You're genuinely ready for retirement. Start planning your exit strategy and get excited about what's next.

If you scored in the middle third:

You're getting there, but you need focused preparation. Give yourself 6-12 months to work on weak areas. Don't rush—retirement isn't going anywhere.

If you scored in the bottom third:

You need significant preparation time, possibly 1-2 years. This isn't bad news; it's a gift. Now you know exactly what to work on, and you have time to do it right.

Your Personal Action Plan

Based on your assessment results, here's what to focus on:

If Identity Readiness is your weakness:

- Start introducing yourself without your job title
- Develop three non-work ways to describe yourself
- Join groups based on interests, not profession
- Timeline: Start at once, practice daily

If Social Readiness is your weakness:

- Join a new group or club this month
- Reconnect with old friends outside work
- Start building relationships that will survive retirement
- Timeline: Begin now, retirement won't create friends for you

If Purpose Readiness is your weakness:

- Find three ways to contribute without earning money
- Explore volunteer opportunities
- Consider what legacy you want to create
- Timeline: Start exploring 2 years before retirement

If Relationship Readiness is your weakness:

- Schedule the difficult conversations with your spouse
- Discuss expectations, fears, and hopes openly
- Consider couples counseling if needed
- Timeline: Critical to address 1 year before retirement

If these assessments showed you're not ready, that's not failure—that's clarity. You now know exactly what to work on. Start preparing now, even if retirement seems years away. Because when that day comes—whether by choice or circumstance—you want to be ready for all of it, not just the financial part.

CHAPTER 2

Your Last Year of Work

*"There is a whole new kind of life ahead, full of experiences
just waiting to happen. Some call it 'retirement.' I call it bliss."*
— Betty Sullivan

You know what the people who retired the right way had? Time. They got a whole year to wrap things up. They'd hand off projects bit by bit. Train whoever was taking over their work. And mentally? They could start letting go. Start thinking of themselves as someone who used to do that job, not someone who still does it.

They gradually got used to the idea. They'd practice talking about themselves at events without defaulting to their work title. They could even test it out, take a Thursday afternoon off, and see what it feels like not to be in meetings. See if they liked it.

My 'final year' was three days of boxing up office supplies and trying not to cry in front of the security guard who watched me turn in my badge. No gradual transition, no time to adjust to the idea, no practice runs. Just employed on Monday, retired by Friday, and wondering what had just happened to my life.

Test Driving Your Future

You shouldn't rush into retirement. But you also can't analyze every scenario forever. At some point, you've got to make the call.

If you know your retirement date—whether it's next month or next year—you can test drive this massive life change while you still have a job to return to if you discover you're not ready. You can experiment with retirement schedules during vacations, have those awkward but necessary conversations with your spouse while work stress isn't clouding everything, and figure out who you want to be after your business cards go in the recycling. The **Test Drive Manual** at the end of this chapter gives you specific ways to practice. Use them. I promise you, practicing retirement while employed beats learning it all the hard way.

The Unexpected Emotions Nobody Warns You About

During what turned out to be my final year, though I didn't know it, I experienced emotions I wasn't prepared for. Talking with others who had more traditional transitions, I've learned these feelings are universal, whether your retirement is planned or sudden.

Short-Timer's Syndrome hits once you've mentally checked out. For those who know they're leaving, this can last months. Every meeting feels pointless. Every new initiative seems irrelevant. You're physically present but mentally already gone.

Legacy Panic struck me hardest. With only three days, I couldn't document and create guides for processes that I only knew. I spent what time I had with my closest colleague, who had been my daily partner for years, making sure she had the knowledge she'd need. Those with longer runways often spend months on legacy projects, desperate to cement their contributions before becoming yesterday's news.

Premature nostalgia often takes us by surprise. We start to feel sentimental about things we used to complain about. Those dull conference calls served as the foundation for us to become a team. The manager who repeatedly asked the same questions became someone who helped me develop my patience. Even the awful coffee turns into something we'll miss.

Survivor's Guilt is real, especially if you're choosing to leave while colleagues must continue. I thought being laid off would spare me this, but I felt guilty about my generous severance when others got nothing. For those choosing retirement, watching stressed coworkers while you're planning your escape can be emotionally complicated.

The Weird Psychology of Letting Go

Here's what nobody tells you about the final year: you're grieving while you're still alive. You're mourning a career that defined you for decades while that career is still happening. It's like attending your own professional funeral.

I don't remember much about those three days. My mother's funeral was two weeks before, and I was still - I don't know. Was I grieving for her? The job? Both? I couldn't separate it. Everything hurt.

I sat there deleting emails. Thousands of them. Years and years of conversations that suddenly didn't matter anymore. And the whole time, my brain wouldn't shut up. Can we afford this? What happens when the severance runs out? What if Ed gets sick? I was about to be 69 years old. Nobody's hiring someone my age. Nobody.

Delete files. Clear the browser history. Take the personal photos off my desktop. Hand back the laptop, hand in the badge. I wasn't thinking about my legacy, whether I'd had an influence, or any of that. I just wanted to get through it. Get out. My brain kept switching between feeling completely numb and straight-up panic.

At my age, I was too old to find another job, and I wouldn't put myself through that for just one year, anyway. While colleagues with longer runways might spend months on legacy projects, I spent my three days just trying to exit cleanly, with my mind cycling between mourning my mother and terrifying money calculations.

For those with longer transitions, this grief plays out differently. Some people mentally check out a year early, coasting through their final months. Others work harder than ever, trying to squeeze every last drop of meaning from their career. Both responses are normal. Both are forms of processing loss.

The mental shift happens in stages, and you can't rush it. First comes denial—this isn't really happening. Then anger—at the company, the timing, the unfairness. Then bargaining—maybe I could consult, maybe part-time work would be better. Then depression—what's the point of any of this? Finally, acceptance—this chapter is ending, and that's okay.

The Strategic Exit: Leaving on Your Terms (If You Get to Choose)

I didn't get to orchestrate my exit, but watching colleagues who did taught me valuable lessons about leaving well. Your final year isn't just about wrapping up—it's about setting yourself up for what comes next.

The Knowledge Transfer should begin at least 6 months in advance. Document your processes, but more importantly, document your thinking. Anyone can follow the steps; understanding why those steps matter is what makes someone truly ready to take over. I had three days and didn't have time to download decades of knowledge.

The Relationship Transition requires intentionality. Start strengthening connections with people you want to keep as friends, while gracefully distancing from toxic relationships you're happy to leave behind. Exchange personal contact information early—by the time you're cleaning out your desk, it's too late for natural relationship building. The **Test Drive Manual** includes specific exercises for testing which work relationships will survive retirement.

The Legacy Project deserves thought. Choose one significant contribution to complete before you leave. Make it something visible, valuable, and unquestionably yours. This isn't about ego—it's about closure. You need to know you mattered, that your years meant something. For me, this became my retirement book—my unexpected legacy project.

Announcing Your Retirement: The Timing Tightrope

People will tell you to give plenty of notice before you retire. Months. I don't think that's always the right move.

I watched a colleague do this. She announced her retirement would be in eight months. She thought she was being considerate, giving them time to plan.

Big mistake. They basically treated her as if she were already gone and stopped including her in strategic planning. In addition, they assigned interesting projects to others. She spent her last eight months feeling completely sidelined, as if she didn't matter anymore, even though she was still showing up every day.

Her last few months there were lonely. Really lonely. The organization had already moved on without her. So, giving notice is complicated. There's no perfect way to do it.

Announcing too late (less than two weeks) burns bridges. Unless you're in a hostile situation, this approach leaves resentment that can follow you into retirement. References disappear, networking connections evaporate, and your professional reputation takes an unnecessary hit.

The sweet spot seems to be 2-3 months—enough time for transition planning without becoming irrelevant. This gives you time to wrap up projects, train replacements, and leave gracefully without enduring months as a lame duck.

Of course, I got three days' notice, which made all of this moot. If retirement is forced on you suddenly, focus on practical matters first, emotional processing second, and legacy concerns last. You can't control the timing, but you can control your response.

The Art of Training Your Replacement (Even If You Don't Have One)

Whether you're training a specific person or just documenting for whoever comes next, this process is more emotional than you expect. You're essentially teaching someone to be you—or at least, to do what you did. It's intimate and strange.

If you have an actual replacement to train, remember they don't want to be you; they want to be themselves in your role. Share knowledge without expecting them to replicate your approach. This is harder than it sounds when you've done something successfully for years.

Test Driving While You Still Can

One gift of knowing your retirement date: you can practice retirement before it's permanent. The complete **Test Drive Manual** in Toolkit

#2 at the end of this chapter provides detailed approaches, but here's what I wish I'd done:

I wish I'd taken a "retirement" sabbatical—even just two weeks—to experience life without work while still employed. I wish I'd practiced introducing myself without my title. I wish I'd tested whether my marriage could manage unlimited togetherness. I wish I'd known which work friendships were real.

The Slow Fade vs. The Clean Break

You basically have two ways to leave your job: ease out slowly or make a clean exit. Some people start checking out months before their last day. They cut back on their hours, hand off responsibilities, and begin mentally distancing themselves from their work. Others stay all-in right up until they walk out the door for the last time. Neither approach is right or wrong, but knowing which one fits you matters.

Friends who went for the slow fade experienced mixed results. Some loved it - they dialed back their hours, started building their retirement life while still collecting a paycheck and keeping one foot in their professional identity. But just as many found it agonizing. They weren't really working, but they weren't really retired either. Just stuck in limbo.

I got the clean break by default - laid off Tuesday, done by Friday. Was it a shock? Absolutely. But there was also something clarifying about it. No dragging it out, no watching myself become less and less relevant. Just done.

There's no right way to do this. But that slow fade-out? It's harder than you'd think.

You're still showing up every day, but you're watching other people do the work you used to do. They're making decisions without asking you. Your opinion used to matter - now it's optional. They can take it or leave it.

That hurts. It's a weird kind of hurt, too. You're not fired or pushed out, but you're also not really needed anymore. And you know it. Everyone knows it.

Your Last Day: Making It Count

My last day was chaotic, driving an hour to the office, boxing up possessions, handing in my laptop and badge, and saying rushed goodbyes. If you get to plan yours, make it intentional.

Take photos, but not just of things—of moments. The morning light in your office. Your name on the door. The view you've looked at for years. These seem silly now, but become precious later.

Three days. So, my goodbyes were a mess. I didn't get to say half of what I wanted to tell people.

If you get time to plan your exit - and I hope you do - actually tell people what they meant to you. Not the usual stuff like "it's been great working with you." Tell them what they really meant to you, saying things like "you made me laugh when I wanted to quit," or "that advice you gave me about the promotion? It changed everything," or "when my mom was dying, you checked on me every single day, and I never forgot that."

I've seen people do this right. My friend Janet brought cookies to everyone in her department. Homemade ones. And she wrote little notes - not generic ones, but specific memories she had with each person. Another guy I knew left his coffee mug in the break room when he retired. It had these terrible accounting jokes on it, and he loved that stupid mug. He put a sign on it: "May it bring someone else their morning smile."

Me? I sent a group email. I wrote it in about ten minutes and hit send, and I still hate that I did it that way.

Don't do what I did. You deserve better than that. The people you worked with deserve better than that.

The Gap Between Ending and Beginning

There's a period between your last day of work and your first real day of retirement. For me, it was sixteen weeks of severance—still getting paid but not working. It's a strange limbo.

Use this gap wisely. It's tempting to treat it like an extended vacation, but it's actually precious preparation time. This is when you should be doing the exercises in the **Test Drive Manual**, having difficult conversations with your spouse, and beginning to build your new routine.

I wasted much of my gap period in denial and depression. The **Test Drive Manual** will help you use this time productively, whether you have sixteen weeks as I did or just a long weekend.

What I Wish Someone Had Told Me

I didn't get a final year, but watching colleagues who did taught me something important: that last year of work isn't really about work anymore. It's about letting go. You're still showing up, still producing, still attending meetings, but underneath all that regular activity, you're quietly becoming someone else. The person who needed that title, that office, that sense of being essential—that person is starting to fade, making room for whoever comes next.

I cried in my car after I turned in my badge. Not pretty crying either - the kind where you can't see because your glasses fog up, and afterwards, you're just wiped out.

I was very upset. Eight years at this company and a career of forty-five years, and it's just - gone. Like I was nothing, and I was scared about money, even though our financial planner kept saying we'd be fine. I couldn't make myself believe it.

But there was something else too, under the anger and the fear. It felt like grief. Like someone died. Which sounds dramatic, but that's what it felt like. Except that the person who died was me. Not the me me, but the work me. The director me. That person was just... gone.

For months, I thought these feelings meant I was managing retirement poorly. Now I know better. You're supposed to grieve at the end of a career that defined you for decades. You're supposed to feel afraid of the unknown. If you don't feel these things, you probably weren't very invested in your work to begin with. The feelings aren't weakness—they're evidence that your work mattered to you. And despite what it feels like in those dark moments in your car, they do fade. Not quickly, not wholly, but enough that you can build something new in the space they leave behind.

Most importantly, how you leave matters less than you think. Whether you get a grand farewell or a sudden goodbye, whether you train a successor or leave notes for a stranger, whether you fade slowly or break cleanly—these details feel monumentally important at the time but fade quickly in retirement.

What matters is that you begin preparing for what's next while dealing with what's ending. The **Test Drive Manual** that follows will help you do exactly that.

Before moving to Chapter 3, spend time with the **Test Drive Manual**. Try at least one approach—the Weekend Test Run if nothing else. You're going to need this stuff when we get to Chapter 3, where we talk about the identity crisis part. Trust me on that one.

•

Toolkit #2
The Retirement Test Drive Manual

Think of it like test-driving a car before you buy it. You wouldn't buy a vehicle you'll drive for the next 30 years without sitting in it first, would you? Start with simple exercises and work up to the complex ones.

Test Drive #1: The Weekend Test Run

Start with this one. It's simple, and you'll learn more in two days than you would from a dozen retirement books.

Friday Night Preparation:

The second you leave work on Friday, you're "retired" until Monday morning. That means:
- Work devices off
- Work stuff put away
- No "just checking" your email
- Tell your family what you're doing
- No tackling that project list (that's cheating - retirement isn't about being productive)

Saturday - The Honeymoon:

Wake up without an alarm. Notice when you woke up without the alarm.
- How long did it take before you felt restless?

- When did that guilt about "doing nothing" creep in?

  ____

- What did you actually want to do with your time?

  ____

- And be honest - how many times did work pop into your head?

  ____

That evening, jot down three things you noticed. Keep it to observations, not judgments. "I felt anxious by 10 AM" - that's an observation. "I'm terrible at relaxing" - that's a judgment, and it's not helpful.

Your three things:

____

____

____

Sunday - The Reality:

The novelty's worn off by Sunday. This is where it gets real. Watch for:
- Do you still get the Sunday scaries when there's no Monday deadline looming?

  ____

- Are you fighting the urge to prep for Monday out of habit?

  ____

- How do you feel about facing another unstructured day? Excited? Dreading it?

  ____

- What do you wish you were doing instead?

____

Sunday evening, be honest with yourself or your partner. Could I do this every day for the next 30 years? _________________

Monday Morning Reflection:

Before you head back to work on Monday, write down:
- What surprised you most?

____

- What was more difficult than you thought?

____

- What was better than you expected?

____

- What would need to change to make this work long-term?

____

- Are you relieved to go back to work, or sad about it?

____

Test Drive #2: The Mock Schedule Exercise

One of my biggest shocks was the complete absence of structure. This exercise helps you discover what kind of structure you actually want, rather than what you think you should want.

Week 1: The Structured Approach

Create a detailed retirement schedule:
- 7:00 AM - Wake up, coffee, newspaper
- 8:00 AM - Exercise

- 9:30 AM - Shower, dress
- 10:00 AM - Project time
- 12:00 PM - Lunch
- 1:00 PM - Volunteer work
- 3:00 PM - Errands
- 5:00 PM - Dinner prep
- 6:00 PM - Dinner
- 7:00 PM - Evening activity
- 10:00 PM - Bed

Live this for one whole week (use vacation time if possible, or just evenings and weekends).

What you'll likely discover: This much structure in retirement feels like prison.

Week 2: The Unstructured Approach

No schedule at all. Wake up when you want. Do what feels right in the moment—complete freedom.

What you'll likely discover: This feels great for about two days, then the anxiety kicks in.

Week 3: Finding Your Sweet Spot

Based on what you learned, create just enough structure to hold the day up:
- Morning routine (time flexible)
- One scheduled commitment
- Lunch at an actual table
- Afternoon flexibility
- Evening wind-down

This is what most successful retirees land on—structure without rigidity, routine without monotony.

Test Drive #3: The Visualization Exercises

I used to think visualization was woo-woo nonsense. Then I realized that I'd been visualizing retirement for years—I just had it all wrong. My visualizations were all highlights: travel, leisure, freedom. I never visualized Tuesday afternoon in February when it's raining, and I'm alone.

Exercise 1: The Daily Life Visualization

Set aside 30 minutes. Close your eyes and visualize a completely ordinary Tuesday in retirement, six months from now.

Walk through the entire day in detail:
- You wake up. What time? How do you feel?

____

- You get out of bed. What's your first thought?

____

- You have breakfast. Where? What? With whom?

____

- It's 9 AM. What are you doing?

____

- It's noon. Where are you? What are you eating?

____

- It's 3 PM. The afternoon stretches ahead. Now what?

____

- It's 6 PM. Dinner time. What's happening?

____

- It's 8 PM. The evening is yours. How do you spend it?

  ____

- Bedtime. How do you feel about today? Tomorrow?

  ____

Be ruthlessly honest. If you can't visualize a random Tuesday, you're not ready.

Exercise 2: The Ideal Day Exercise

Now visualize your ideal retirement day. Not a vacation day—a regular day that you'd be happy to repeat. Include:
- Balance of structure and flexibility
- Mix of solo and social time
- Blend of productivity and leisure
- Physical and mental activity
- Indoor and outdoor elements
- Giving and receiving

Compare this to your ordinary Tuesday visualization. How far apart are they? The gap shows how much work you need to do.

Exercise 3: The Five Senses Retirement

Walk through what retirement will feel like using all five senses.
Sight: What you'll see every day. Your garden as you drink morning coffee?

The inside of a gym? Those same four walls of your house?

____

____

____

Hearing: Will you be trading the office buzz for something else - maybe silence, maybe the TV running all day. Does quiet feel peaceful to you, or does it make you anxious?

____

____

____

Touch: What will your hands be doing? Digging in garden soil? Typing on a keyboard for a hobby project?

____

____

____

Taste: Will you take time for leisurely breakfasts, or grab whatever's easy?

____

____

____

Smell: This one catches people off guard. The smell of coffee brewing in your own kitchen at 9 AM on a Tuesday. Fresh air if you're spending more time outside.

____

____

____

This exercise makes retirement physical and real, not just conceptual.

Exercise 4: The Legacy Visualization

Picture yourself five years into retirement. You're at a party, and someone asks what you've been up to since you stopped working. What do you want to tell them?

Not vague stuff like "oh, you know, enjoying life." I mean real things. Maybe you want to say you wrote a book. Or that you finally learned Spanish. Traveled to ten countries. Became a master gardener. Rebuilt relationships with your kids.

What's your answer? Now work backwards. What needs to happen in Year 1 for those five-year accomplishments to be real?

____

____

____

Exercise 5: The Resource Mapping

Visualize your resources in retirement—not just financial, but all resources:

Time: 2,000+ hours per year you used to spend working. Where will they go?

____

Energy: Without work stress, you might have more. Or without structure, you might have less. Which seems likely?

____

Skills: Which will transfer? Which will atrophy? Which new ones will you need?

____

Relationships: Who will remain? Who will fade? Who will appear?

____

Space: Where will you spend your days? Is your home ready for you to be there all the time?

____

Purpose: What will replace your work achievements? What will make you feel valuable?

Exercise 6: The Seasonal Planning

Visualize each season of your first retirement year:

Spring: New beginnings. What will you start?

Summer: Full bloom. What will you be doing daily?

Fall: Harvest time. What will you accomplish?

Winter: Reflection period. How will you manage the quiet months?

Different seasons bring different challenges.

Test Drive #4: The Preretirement Sabbatical

This is the gold standard of retirement test drives.

Take 2-4 weeks off consecutively
- Live on your retirement budget
- Follow your planned retirement schedule
- No contact with work
- No vacation activities—live like it's permanent

Week 1: The Honeymoon

Everything feels great. Document daily:
- Energy levels
- Mood
- Activities
- Social interactions
- Anxiety levels
- Satisfaction ratings

Week 2: The Crash

This is when reality hits. The novelty is gone. If you're going crazy on Day 10, it's normal. And it's valuable.

Week 3: The Adjustment

You start finding rhythm. You figure out what actually works versus what you thought would work.

What you may discover:
- You need more social interaction than planned
- Unstructured days make you anxious
- You miss problem-solving challenges
- Your marriage needs different boundaries
- Part-time work might be essential

Week 4: The Decision

By Week 4, you have real data.

If You Can't Take A Sabbatical:
- Use all vacation time consecutively
- Take unpaid leave if possible
- At a minimum, use long weekends
- Even a week is valuable

Test Drive #5: The Relationship Stress Test

If you're married or partnered, retirement dramatically changes your relationship. Test it before it's permanent.

The 24/7 Together Test:

Spend an entire week together with no work to escape to. Both of you take time off. Stay home - don't turn this into a vacation. Just live your regular life, except you're both there, all day, every day.

You'll figure out pretty quickly:
- Who needs more space

  ____

- Whose morning routine drives the other one crazy

  ____

- Whether your house actually has enough room for two people who aren't leaving for work

  ____

- How much togetherness feels good versus suffocating

  ____

- What boundaries must be set before retirement starts

  ____

The Conversation Prompts:

During your test week, discuss:
- How will mornings work?

  ____

- Who cooks when?

  ____

- How much time together/apart?

  ____

- What are our needs for individual space?

  ____

- Who's managing what around the house?

  ____

- How are we managing money once the paychecks stop?

  ____

- What do each of us expect our social life to look like?

  ____

- Do we both actually want to travel?

  ____

These conversations may feel awkward. Have them anyway.

Your Test Drive Action Plan

Month 1:
- Complete Weekend Test Run
- Start Visualization Exercises

Month 2:
- Try Mock Schedule Exercise
- Continue visualizations

Month 3:

- Relationship Stress Test
- Map resources

Month 4-6:

- Take a Preretirement Sabbatical (or longest possible break)
- Evaluate all results
- Adjust retirement plan accordingly

Every test drive you do increases your chances of retirement success. Test everything. Practice retirement while you still have a job to return to. Your test drives might reveal you're completely ready, or they might show you need more preparation. Either outcome is a success because it's based on experience, not assumption.

The Research Behind My Experience

I'm not just suggesting you test drive retirement because it sounds like a good idea. There's solid research backing this up.

AARP conducted a comprehensive 2022 study of people who "practiced being retired" for at least 2 weeks before they retired. Those people made 65% fewer major mistakes in their first year than those who just jumped straight in. That's a huge difference.

The Mayo Clinic published a report on healthy aging and daily rhythms. They found that when people tested out retirement schedules before retiring, it cut the time to establish sustainable routines from six months to six weeks. Six weeks instead of six months - that alone makes it worth doing.

MoneySense conducted research in 2023 that delved deeper into what happens when you test-drive retirement. They found that people made significant changes to their plans based on what they learned. 42% adjusted their budget expectations. 38% modified how they thought they'd structure their days. And 31% realized they'd need part-time work for their mental health, not because they needed the money.

The National Institute on Aging studied healthy transitions and they found that just doing the "weekend experiment" - where you simulate a retirement weekend - helped retirees identify 80% of their significant adjustment challenges before they even retired.

CHAPTER 3

The Identity Crisis

"For many, retirement is a time for personal growth,
which becomes the path to greater freedom."
— Robert Delamontague

Who Are You Without Your Business Card?

For 45 years, when someone asked, "What do you do?" I had my answer ready: "I'm a director at..." It rolled off my tongue like my own name.

Then I got the phone call in April. Position eliminated. And just like that, I didn't know how to answer that question anymore. The professional version of me—the one I'd built my entire adult life—was gone.

What I didn't realize was that I wasn't just leaving a job. I was walking away from one of the most powerful identities I'd ever built, and my brain wasn't ready to let it go. The identity crisis that follows retirement isn't a maybe—it's a certainty. The only variable is how prepared you are to face it.

The Neuroscience of Why This Hurts So Much

Let me explain what's actually happening in your brain when you retire, because understanding the science helped me realize I wasn't weak or broken—I was experiencing neurological withdrawal.

Think about nailing a big project at work—praise from your boss or hitting your quarterly goals. Every single time, your brain lit up with dopamine. You wanted more of it. And when you worked side-by-side with your team and built those relationships, oxytocin flooded your system. Your title and that director's office you'd earned mattered, and along with the respect you'd built over decades, all triggered serotonins. Even the stress pumped adrenaline through you, keeping you sharp.

For decades, your brain got used to this chemical cocktail. It came to expect it and depend on it. So, when work disappears, it's not just that your calendar looks empty. Your brain's entire reward system gets thrown off balance.

That's why it hurt so much. I wasn't just sad about losing my job. My brain was literally grieving the loss of its daily chemical rewards while trying to figure out why the achievement factory had suddenly shut down. Understanding this didn't make the withdrawal easier, but at least I stopped thinking I was weak for feeling so empty. I was just chemically dependent on being needed, and nobody sells a patch for that.

The Research Behind My Experience

That identity crisis that blindsided me? It's not just in my head. It's an actual documented psychological phenomenon.

The American Psychological Association did research in 2022 on career transitions. What they found is striking - losing your professional identity triggers the same grief responses in your brain as losing a loved one—the same reactions. So, when I felt like I was grieving my director title, I actually was grieving it in a very real, neurological way.

The Journal of Gerontology published a 2022 study on stress and role transitions that further explored this. They measured cortisol and dopamine levels in new retirees and found they mirrored those of people undergoing clinical withdrawal—actual withdrawal, like from a substance.

For high-achieving professionals specifically, the study found these effects last an average of six months. Six months of your brain chemistry being out of whack.

Those first few weeks, I thought I was losing my mind. I'd wake up panicking. I couldn't think straight. And I kept beating myself up about it - why was I being so weak? So dramatic?

Turns out I wasn't being either. I was in withdrawal. My brain had been running on work-related dopamine hits for 45 years. That supply got cut off overnight.

Understanding this doesn't make it easier, but it does make sense.

The Identity Fusion Timeline

Now I realize exactly when the shift happened—when I stopped being someone who had a job and started being my job. It didn't happen overnight. It was more like gaining weight; you don't notice it day by day until suddenly your clothes don't fit.

The first few years of work? It was just a paycheck. I was figuring out how to be an adult, and work was part of that, but it wasn't me. I had other things going on. Friends who had nothing to do with my job. Hobbies. Plans that didn't involve work at all.

But then things changed. I don't know precisely when. Maybe around ten years in? I started noticing I'd go to parties and talk about work like it was the most interesting thing happening in my life. My Sunday nights got bad, but not in the usual way. I wasn't dreading Monday. I was thinking about quarterly reports that were weeks away.

It got worse. By the time I'd been there fifteen, twenty years, people introduced me by my title. Even Ed did it. "This is my wife, Cheryl; she's a director at..." Like the job was part of my actual name. I never decided that. It just happened.

And by the end? I couldn't tell anymore where work stopped, and I started. My dreams were about work. My friends were from work. What I worried about, what I was proud of - all work. It wasn't "work-life balance." It was just life.

The fusion was so complete that when that April phone call came, they weren't just cutting a position; they were cutting a person. They were erasing half of who I'd become.

Most of us don't notice this happening. It's gradual, invisible, until separation feels like losing a limb. When someone asked about me, I'd talk about work projects, challenges, and successes. Even my hobbies got squeezed into "when I have time after work." My identity had been hijacked so slowly that I never saw it coming.

High-Identity Careers: When It's Even Harder

Certain professions become so deeply intertwined with personal identity that retirement feels especially traumatic. Doctors, lawyers, academics, executives, these aren't just jobs, they're callings that define not just what you do but who you are.

I have a physician friend who couldn't imagine life without "Dr." before his name. Even after retiring, he continued giving lectures at conferences and auditing medical charts for the state association. He wasn't seeing patients, but he found a way to keep his professional identity on his own terms. That gradual disengagement worked for him.

For me, the abrupt ending meant I had to find other ways to manage the transition. Remember the **Identity Readiness Pillar** from Toolkit #1? If you scored low there, this chapter is especially crucial for you.

The Digital Identity Dilemma

Nobody warned me about this part. What do you do with your LinkedIn profile?

Mine had said "Director at..." for years. Now what? Do I delete it? Change it to "Retired"?

I sat there staring at that profile for like twenty minutes. "Retired" felt like giving up. Like announcing to everyone, "I'm done, I'm irrelevant now, move along."

My LinkedIn headline. I must have stared at that blank box for an hour. What do you even say? I typed and deleted about fifteen versions before settling on "Former Director, Current Explorer of Life's Next Chapter." Weak, but whatever. At least it was honest.

My work email was shut down. Those professional newsletters I'd relied on for years? They didn't follow me to my personal account. And the online forums where I used to jump in with advice? They kept right on going. Turns out they didn't need me.

Every time another digital connection died, the message was clear: you don't matter here anymore.

I found myself obsessively checking my personal email and looking for what, exactly? I don't know. Something that felt like the validation I used to get from work.

Beginning to Imagine Yourself Beyond the Title

The most challenging question in early retirement is: "Who am I when I'm not working?" For weeks, I couldn't answer it. I'd start sentences with "I used to..." and trail off into uncomfortable silence. The present tense felt impossible.

Here's what finally helped me start reimagining myself:

Rediscovering my core self. I had to think back to who I was before I was a director. What drew my interest before my demanding career took over? What values remained constant throughout my life? Slowly, I remembered: I was creative (hence the knitting and sewing), I was a caregiver (raising triplets and giving weekend care for my mother taught me that), I was a learner (always reading or taking online courses, always curious).

Exploring dormant interests. I'd set aside so many of my interests to my demanding career. Writing—not reports or presentations, but real writing about real life. Creating with my hands. Teaching, but not in conference rooms—teaching people about retirement transition. These interests had been waiting patiently for decades.

Recognizing my other roles. I was already doing many things beyond being a director. Wife to Ed. Mother to triplets. Sister to my Wednesday lunch companion. Neighbor, friend, amateur knitter, unpracticed but enthusiastic bread baker. These roles didn't disappear with my job—they were waiting to expand.

Simple Exercises That Actually Help

Instead of wallowing in identity confusion, I developed exercises to help me reconnect with who I am beyond my job title. These aren't separate from your daily life; you can do them while having coffee, taking a walk, or lying awake at 3 AM (which you probably are anyway).

The Role Audit: List twenty things you are in life—not job titles, but roles—parent, friend, gardener, reader, walker, dreamer, helper, learner. Circle the ones that continue in retirement. Those circled items? That's your core identity, the parts that transcend any business card.

About a month into retirement, my sister asked me to try something. 'Write down what you are,' she said, 'but you can't use anything work-related.' I sat there with my pen frozen. Without 'Director' or 'professional' or even 'colleague,' who was I?

It took me an embarrassingly long time to come up with twenty things. Mother—that was easy. Wife to Ed. Sister. But then what? I started grasping: A Person who reads mysteries. Woman who knits and sews. Someone who makes a good pot roast. A friend who gives away her knitted items. Enthusiastic singer in the church choir.

When I looked at my list, I noticed something. Most of these things had survived my entire career, tucked into the margins of my work life. They were still there, waiting. The job had taken up so much space that I'd forgotten about these quieter parts of myself. But there they were—the parts of Cheryl that no employer could eliminate with a phone call.

That messy, random list of roles turned out to be more stable than any business card I'd ever carried. Jobs end. But being someone who makes good pot roast and gives away everything she knits? That's apparently forever.

The Value Discovery: Ask yourself what you'd do for free, what problems in the world upset you most, and what achievements would matter even if no one knew about them. For me, it was helping others navigate major life transitions, fighting against ageism in the workplace, and creating things with my hands. These values didn't retire when I did.

The Story Test: Tell your life story in five minutes. Notice how much it revolves around work. Then ask: What else defines me? What makes me proud that has nothing to do with my career? My story was embarrassingly work-heavy at first. Now it includes raising triplets, supporting Ed's presidency of the floral association, creating my craft room sanctuary, and writing this book.

The Unexpected Identity Gifts

Here's what nobody tells you: losing your work identity, as painful as it is, creates space for parts of you that have been dormant for decades. I'm discovering aspects of Cheryl that Director Cheryl never had time to explore.

I'm funnier when I'm not worried about professional appropriateness. I'm more creative when I'm not exhausted from meetings. I'm a better wife when I'm not distracted by tomorrow's presentation. I'm more myself when I'm not performing a professional role.

The identity crisis is real, and it hurts. But it's also an opportunity to become more than your job title ever allowed you to be. You're not losing yourself—you're uncovering yourself.

Moving Forward Without Looking Back

Six months into retirement, when someone asked me what I do, I didn't say, for the first time, "I used to be a director." I said, "I'm writing a book about retirement, I sing in my church choir, and I'm learning to make artisan bread—badly."

The person laughed and said, "That sounds like a full life."

And you know what? It is. It's different from my director life, less prestigious perhaps, but it's mine. All mine. No performance reviews, no organizational charts, no politics—just me, figuring out who Cheryl is when she's not trying to be anything for anyone else.

The identity crisis doesn't resolve overnight. You don't wake up one morning with a fully formed new identity. It develops slowly, day by day, choice by choice. Every time you introduce yourself without your former title, every time you find joy in something that has nothing to do with career achievement, every time you realize you matter for who you are rather than what you did, you're building your new identity.

The Bottom Line on Identity

You spent decades becoming your professional self. Give yourself at least months—maybe years—to discover your retirement self. This isn't a failure of character or a sign of weakness. It's a massive psychological transition that deserves respect, patience, and compassion, especially from yourself.

Eight months ago, I thought losing my job meant losing myself. Turns out, what I lost was Director Cheryl—the woman who knew exactly what to do at 9 AM on a Tuesday. The one with business cards and a director-sized office. The one who called and led meetings.

That person is gone. And honestly? I still miss her sometimes.

But what surprised me? Underneath all that professional armor was someone I'd forgotten about.

I write notes to myself and leave them scattered everywhere. I watch the same Jane Austen movies on repeat without guilt. At 69, I decided to teach myself to make artisan bread. Every loaf looks like a deflated football, and I'm okay with that.

This person was there all along, patiently waiting through forty-five years of job titles and performance reviews.

I still feel lost sometimes. Last week I was at church, and someone asked what I do. I completely stumbled over it. Just stood there like an idiot.

I'm starting to understand something. I mean, I'm still working on it. I don't have this figured out yet.

When you're rebuilding who you are at this age, you're not becoming someone new. At least I don't think so. It's more like... you're finding parts of yourself that were always there. But they got covered up. Buried under decades of work and deadlines, and being whoever your job needed you to be.

Forty-five years is a long time to push parts of yourself aside.

Every small discovery—that I like morning walks when I'm not rushing to work, that I'm funnier when I'm not trying to be professional, that I can learn new things without needing them for my career-these aren't reinventions. They're excavations.

The identity crisis is real, and it hurts. But it's also temporary. And the person you find on the other side might be someone you like better than the one you lost.

Turn to Chapter 4 to learn how to navigate the crucial first 30 days of retirement, when the identity crisis meets daily reality.

CHAPTER 4

Days 1-30 - Your Survival Guide

"Retire from work, but not from life."

— M.K. Soni

Day One: The Overwhelming Freedom

I'll never forget my first Monday morning as a retired person. My alarm didn't go off at 5:45 AM because I'd turned it off—permanently, I thought. I woke up at 7:23 AM in a panic, thinking I'd overslept. Then reality hit: I had nowhere to be. Ever.

That should feel liberating, right? Instead, I sat on the edge of my bed for twenty minutes, completely paralyzed. What do you DO when you can do anything?

I made coffee slowly, savoring, not rushing. Then I sat with that coffee and realized I had eight more hours to fill before it was socially acceptable to go to bed. The euphoria everyone talks about? It lasted exactly three sips of coffee before the anxiety set in.

The **Days 1-30 Survival Templates** at the end of this chapter will give you specific daily guidance for navigating these first crucial weeks. I created them from my own trial-and-error experience, and I wish I'd had them on Day One.

Week One: The Fake Vacation That Isn't

The first week feels like vacation—except the vacation never ends, and that's when it gets weird.

Days Two and Three felt like a weekend. I slept late, watched the news, and watered the plants. But by Wednesday, my brain started sending distress signals. "Why are we still in weekend mode? Something's wrong!"

My husband asked, "So what are you going to do today?" and I had no answer. The guilt about watching TV at 2 PM was crushing. The overwhelming urge to "be productive" but not knowing where to start.

By Day Four, reality hit. This wasn't a vacation. This was my life now. I stood in the doorway of my spare bedroom, staring at the walk-in closet crammed with yarn—my decades-long stash begging to be organized. Then I thought about the garage that needed decluttering, the shelves of fabric with projects I'd been dreaming about for years, all those sweater patterns I'd collected, and the brioche knitting technique I'd been dying to learn.

I had so many things I wanted to do that I couldn't figure out where to start. So, I did nothing. I just stood there, frozen by possibility. The thought "Did I make a terrible mistake?" played on repeat.

The Physical Shock Nobody Warns You About

Nobody warned me my body would react physically to retirement. By Day Three, I had headaches, insomnia, and felt exhausted despite doing "nothing." Research explained it perfectly: I was going through workplace withdrawal.

Your body's been running on stress hormones for decades. Mine still is, honestly. I wake up at 3 AM with my heart pounding like something terrible is about to happen. Except nothing is. There's no work crisis. My body doesn't know that yet.

And the afternoons? Around 2 PM, I crash hard. That's when the adrenaline used to kick in at work - meetings, deadlines, whatever. Now there's nothing to kick in for, so I just hit a wall.

The eating thing is weird, too. At work, I had structure - lunch at 11:30 or noon, whatever. Now I forget to eat entirely. Then it's 3 PM, and I'm standing in front of the fridge eating cheese right out of the package because I'm starving and I don't even know why.

Here's what I wish someone had told me: this is normal. You're not losing it. Your body ran on work rhythms for decades. It takes time to figure out a new normal.

Week Two: When the Honeymoon Ends

That second Monday destroyed me. The novelty of staying home? Already gone. Meanwhile, my old colleagues were at their desks doing the work I used to do. My phone sat silent—no inbox to refresh.

I was irrelevant. After 45 years of mattering at work, I just... didn't anymore.

I sat at my kitchen island that morning, drinking cold coffee, and thought, "I don't even know who I am anymore."

That week wasn't about boredom—it was about being frozen. I had a million things I wanted to do, but I couldn't make myself start any of them. I watched the morning news for three hours, then looked at the clock: 11 AM. I could reorganize the yarn closet. Sort through the garage. Pull out one of those fabric projects. Learn brioche knitting. But which one? I just sat there, paralyzed by all the possibilities, nine more hours stretching ahead of me.

I made the mistake of checking LinkedIn that Thursday. Everyone was achieving, announcing, and doing. I was in my pajamas at 11 AM, having done... nothing. The comparison was poisonous.

The Dangerous Second Weekend

Your second weekend as a retiree brings an existential crisis. If every day is like a weekend, what makes actual weekends special? I spent that Saturday in a funk, feeling cheated out of the joy weekends used to bring.

My working friends were savoring their precious time off. I was on Day 13 of time off, with infinite more stretching ahead. The weekend had lost its meaning, and with it, the rhythm of my life.

Week Three: The Minimum Structure That Saves Your Sanity

By Week Three, you need structure, or you'll lose your mind. But not too much structure, that defeats the point of retirement. I tried living with zero structure for two weeks. By Day 15, I was miserable.

So, I created what I call my "skeleton schedule", which has just enough bones to hold the day up. Coffee on the back porch at 7:30. Movement of some kind by 9. One errand or appointment at 11. Lunch at 12:30, at the table, not standing at the counter. The key: it's a framework, not a prison.

I discovered my natural rhythm once work wasn't forcing me into an unnatural pattern. I'm brilliant from 7-11 AM, useless from 2-4 PM, and get a second wind at 6 PM. So, I scheduled accordingly. The templates in Toolkits following Chapters 4, 5, and 6 will help you discover your own rhythm.

The Hermit Trap

By Day 19, I realized something disturbing: I hadn't left my house in three days. Not because I couldn't, there was just no reason to. Everything I needed was inside. Food in the fridge, books to read, TV to watch. Ed was out of town, and the Amazon driver had become the only person I'd seen all week, and we didn't exactly chat.

It freaked me out enough that I made myself a rule. I had to talk to someone every day. An actual person. Face to face. Not texting, not a phone call. I had to get dressed, leave the house, and interact with another human being.

Some days I'd drive to CVS for a pack of gum I didn't even need. I'd go inside the bank instead of using the ATM so that I'd have to talk to the teller. On the terrible days, I'd order my coffee at the counter instead of the drive-through. To say three words to the barista. To hear my own voice talking to someone.

I know how that sounds. A 69-year-old woman is driving to CVS to buy gum she doesn't need because she must practice talking to people. But that's where I was.

Isolation sneaks up on you in retirement. One day, you're a social person with colleagues and meetings and lunch companions. Next, you realize you've been having full conversations with the TV, and the mail carrier is starting to look like your best friend. That silly rule might have saved me from disappearing entirely into my house.

Week Four: Taking Stock

At the start of Week Four, I sat at my kitchen island with a notebook, trying to make sense of what was happening to me. Three weeks of retirement behind me, patterns were starting to appear—some good, some awful, some just weird.

Mornings had become my favorite time. That first cup of coffee, when I could actually taste it instead of throwing it back like medicine while driving to work, was pure luxury. And Sunday nights? For the first time in forty years, Sunday was just Sunday, not the dread before Monday. I could watch a movie without my stomach clenching about the week ahead.

But the afternoons were rough. That stretch of time from 2 to 5 PM - I don't even know what happened during those hours. I'd lose time. And then it would be 5 o'clock, and I'd feel useless and foggy, and I couldn't tell you what I'd done.

I'd end up in the kitchen around 2:30, but not because I was hungry. I'd stand in front of the open refrigerator, just staring at the shelves. By 3 PM, I'd lie on the couch, telling myself I'd rest for a few minutes, and then wake up two hours later feeling worse than ever. Those shame naps, you know? Where you wake up and feel guilty for wasting the afternoon?

The brain thing was the strangest part. My mind was still in work mode, looking for problems to solve, strategies to figure out. But now the problems were real and mine: Which closet do I tackle first? Do I start with the yarn or the fabric? Should I finally learn brioche? My brain kept trying to create a project plan, prioritize, strategize— except I'd freeze up before I could do anything.

I had a closet full of yarn I couldn't wait to knit. Shelves of fabric for projects I'd been dreaming about. And what did I do? I bought crossword puzzles. I hate crossword puzzles. Always have. But I wasn't thinking straight. I needed to give my brain something to chew on, so I'd sit there trying to figure out a seven-letter word for "exhausted" or whatever, thinking, "Is this really what I'm doing now? Making up fake problems to solve when I've got real projects I love just sitting there?"

The Motivation Crisis

About a month in, something hit me. Nobody cared if I did absolutely nothing all day. No boss was checking in. No deadline I'd miss. No performance review at the end of the year.

For someone who'd been driven by external expectations for 45 years, this was terrifying. The motivation had to come from inside now, and I didn't know how to generate it.

My sister saved my sanity with simple advice: instead of trying to fill every minute, choose 2-3 things to do each day. When those are done, you're done—no guilt needed. I turned this into my 'Small Wins Board' whiteboard in my kitchen, where I write three tiny goals each morning. Not 'reorganize entire house' but 'fold one load of laundry.' Not 'get in shape' but 'walk to the mailbox.' Accomplishing three small things felt infinitely better than failing at one overwhelming thing.

Day 30: The First Month Revelation

You've survived your first month! This is bigger than it sounds. You've survived the honeymoon crash, the identity crisis, the boredom, the temptation of isolation, and the motivation challenge.

But here's the truth I wish someone had told me: Month Two is actually harder. Month One has novelty. Month Two has reality. The novelty is completely gone. Regret and doubt intensify. Boredom becomes more sophisticated. Identity questions get deeper.

But also—and this is important—you start catching glimpses of who you're becoming.

Complete Toolkit # 3 **Days 1 – 31 Survival Templates** and then continue to Chapter 5, where Month Two brings deeper challenges— and unexpected breakthroughs.

———— • ————

Toolkit #3
Days 1 - 31 Survival Templates

DAYS 1-30: THE SHOCK AND AWE PHASE

WEEK 1: The Fake Vacation (Days 1-7)

Day 1: The First Monday

Your Day 1 Survival Plan:

Morning:
- Wake up naturally (but you probably won't)
- Make coffee or tea slower than you've ever made it
- Sit somewhere different than your usual rushing spot
- Call one person to share how weird this feels

Afternoon:
- Take a walk—any length, any pace
- Do one small house task (emphasis on small)
- Resist the urge to organize everything

Evening:
- Eat dinner at the table
- Write three sentences about how today felt
- Go to bed when tired, not at "bedtime"

What's Normal on Day 1:
- Waking up in panic
- Checking work phone/email repeatedly
- Feeling guilty about everything
- Crying unexpectedly
- Feeling both relieved and terrified
- Wondering if you made a huge mistake

Day 2: The Void Appears

Your Day 2 Survival Plan:

- Notice the urge to check work email
- Identify the weirdest time of day
- Read something that isn't work-related
- Contact a non-work friend
- Make lunch and eat it sitting down
- Acknowledge that this feels like playing hooky

Day 3: Anxiety Spike

Your Day 3 Emergency Protocol:

- Physical movement—anything for 20 minutes
- Call someone who understands
- Avoid making any major decisions
- Limit news consumption
- Do one thing that feels "productive" if you must
- Remember: This anxiety is withdrawal, not wisdom

Day 4-5: The Identity Wobble

Your Identity Crisis Starter Pack:

- Practice introducing yourself without your work title
- Make a list of other things you are (parent, neighbor, reader, etc.)
- Do something you enjoyed before your career took over
- Avoid LinkedIn like the plague
- Connect with someone who knew you before your career

<u>Weekend 1: Confused Territory</u>

- Notice how weekends feel different (or don't)
- Don't feel guilty about doing "nothing"
- But also do something if sitting still is torture
- Check in with working friends (briefly)
- Start thinking about Week 2 structure

<u>Week 2: Reality Hits Hard (Days 8-14)</u>

Day 8: Panic Monday

Your Week 2 Monday Protocol:

- Expect this to be hard; it's statistically the worst day
- Create three small, achievable tasks
- Leave the house for any reason
- Make one appointment for later this week
- Call another retiree if possible

Day 10: Peak Boredom

Your Boredom Survival Kit:

Remember: This is dopamine withdrawal from work achievements
- Start a puzzle, game, or book series
- Visit a library or bookstore
- Begin researching one potential interest
- Make human contact (grocery store counts)

Day 14: Two-Week Assessment

Two-Week Check-In:

- What's been okay? Write down three things

  ____

- What surprised you?

  ____

- What's been the worst part?

  ____

- What caught you completely off guard?

  ____

- Pick one thing to change for week three (make it small)

____

Week 3: Finding Your Footing (Days 15-21)

Day 15: Structure Experiments

Your Minimum Viable Structure:

    Morning Block: _____________________ (coffee, news, movement)

    Afternoon Block: _______________ (errands, projects, social)

    Evening Block: ___________________ (dinner, reading, wind down)

Day 18: Fighting Isolation

Your Anti-Hermit Protocol:

- One face-to-face interaction daily (coffee shop counts)
- Join something that meets weekly
- Schedule lunch with someone
- Volunteer somewhere
- Say yes to invitations

Day 21: Three-Week Milestone

Your Three-Week Check:

- What have you survived so far?

____

- Is anything even slightly easier than Day 1?

____

- What's something you can look forward to next week?

____

- Give yourself credit for not giving up

<u>Week 4: The Routine Emerges (Days 22-30)</u>

Day 25: Signs of Life

Your Progress Markers:

- One consistent daily routine
- One regular weekly activity
- One person you connect with regularly
- One project you're mildly interested in
- One day you didn't hate

Day 28: Preparing For Month Two

Month Two is actually harder than Month One.

Your Month Two Prep:

- Schedule 5 things for next month

  ____

- Plan one adventure (day trip counts)

  ____

- Set one learning goal

  ____

- Identify needed support

  ____

- Lower your expectations significantly

  ____

Day 30: One Month Down

Your One-Month Letter:

Write yourself a letter to open on Day 60:
- How do you feel today?
- What are you proud of getting through?

- What are you afraid of?
- What do you hope happens in the next month?
- Write something encouraging to your future self

Seal it. Put "Open on Day 60" on it.

You've completed the first month. Days 31-60 will test you in different ways.

The Research Behind My Experience

I didn't just make up this 90-day timeline. The Mayo Clinic identified three distinct phases in retirement adjustment, each lasting about 30 days. When I read their findings, it was eerie how closely they matched what I'd just lived through.

The University of Pennsylvania found that new retirees' emotional patterns are predictable—anxiety peaks around Day 8. The worst boredom hits between Days 30 and 40. Things start stabilizing around Day 75.

The National Bureau of Economic Research found that the 90-day mark is a critical threshold. Retirees who make it through the first 90 days without returning to work have an 85% chance of a successful long-term retirement.

What I went through wasn't unique to me. It's what thousands of other retirees have gone through. The research proves it.

CHAPTER 5

Days 31-60 - The Month That Makes or Breaks

"And in the end, it's not the years in your life that count. It's the life in your years."

— Abraham Lincoln

Day 31: The Novelty Is Dead

Month Two began with a thud. Not a crash—that was Week Two. This was worse—a thud of dull, gray ordinariness. I woke up on Day 31 knowing exactly what my day would look like, and the predictability made me want to pull the covers over my head.

The first month felt like an adventure, even when it was hard. Month Two felt like... nothing. Just days stretching endlessly forward with no particular purpose or destination. No more "firsts" to experience. The honeymoon was entirely over. My patterns were becoming ruts. The "Is this it?" feeling dominated everything.

The Sophisticated Boredom of Week Five

Week Five brought something different. Week Two had been panic—' Oh God, what do I do with myself?' This was... I don't even know what to call it. People talk about retirement boredom, but that wasn't what I felt. I had too much I wanted to do, not too little. The freedom I'd dreamed about for years had become a burden because I couldn't figure out how to use it. By Day 33, I finally understood why some people go back to work six months after retiring. They need to matter. I couldn't imagine why someone would want to go back to work. Now I get it.

I spent an entire Tuesday pulling out knitting patterns, looking at them, and putting them back. Then I'd walk to the yarn closet, stare at the shelves, and walk away without touching anything. Wednesday, I dismantled my craft room setup—the one I'd spent months perfecting while working—convinced the table should face north instead of south. It didn't make any difference. Thursday, I fell into an internet rabbit hole researching espresso machines, reading reviews, comparing features, and creating spreadsheets. Three hours later, I realized I don't even drink espresso.

My brain wouldn't stop. It kept running and running, looking for things to fix. Because that's what it's used to doing, right? It needs problems. So, when there weren't any real problems, it just started making them up.

The fabric bolts on the shelves in my craft room suddenly needed to be organized by fabric type instead of color. Maybe we should investigate switching lawn care providers. I'd spend an hour researching lawn care companies we didn't need to switch to. I'd pull out knitting patterns, look at them, put them back, then do it again the next day. Why? Because my brain was desperate for something to do. Something that felt productive. Something that mattered.

Except none of it mattered. Not really.

The Research Behind My Experience

If you experience boredom in Month Two? It's not a character flaw or a sign that something's wrong with you. It's neurological.

King's College London looked at this too, back in 2023. They studied cognitive adjustment in retirement and gave a name to what I was experiencing: "purpose void syndrome." Your brain is trying to figure out how to feel meaningful without work telling it what matters. The study found it takes about 45 to 60 days for your brain to start building new reward pathways - new ways of feeling accomplished that aren't tied to your job.

So, when I found myself reorganizing my fabric shelves on Day 42 to feel like I'd done something useful? That wasn't me being pathetic. My brain was literally rewiring itself. It was looking for new ways to feel productive since the old work pathways no longer existed.

If I'd known this was happening, I wouldn't have panicked so much. I would've understood it was a normal phase, not my new permanent reality.

Day 35: My Lowest Point

By the end of week five, that's when the doubt really increased. Every person I ran into who was still working seemed to matter. They had somewhere to be. Something important to do. I felt like I was playing at life while they were living it.

Day 35 was my lowest point. I went to LinkedIn and looked at job postings. Not seriously—but seriously enough to scare myself. Was I so weak that I couldn't manage five weeks of freedom?

The answer, I realized later, was that I wasn't weak—I was withdrawing from achievement addiction, from external validation, from decades of work-imposed purpose. This withdrawal peaks around Day 35 and gradually decreases thereafter. You're not failing. You're detoxing.

The Research Behind My Experience

When I hit rock bottom around Day 35, I genuinely thought I was the only person who couldn't figure out retirement. It turns out I was wrong.

The University of Toronto did a study in 2023 on retirement adjustment. They tracked 1,200 new retirees and found that days 30 to 40 are consistently the absolute lowest point in the retirement transition. 73% of people reported that their worst day fell somewhere in that window. Day 35 wasn't just hard for me - it's hard for almost everyone.

For those of us who didn't choose to retire - who got laid off or forced out - it's even worse. Boston College's Center for Retirement Research found that involuntary retirees like me experience 40% more adjustment difficulty than people who chose their own retirement timing. And it takes us an average of six months longer to stabilize. Six months longer of feeling lost and struggling.

Would knowing this research have made Day 35 easier? Probably not. That day was going to be terrible no matter what. But it would have helped me understand that I wasn't broken or a failure. I was right on schedule. This was normal, even though it felt anything but normal at the time.

Week Six: Things Started to Shift

Around day 40, something changed. I didn't even notice it at first.

I woke up one morning and didn't immediately start thinking, "Okay, how am I going to get through today?" I made my coffee. That was it. Just made coffee. Not "made coffee while feeling terrible about my life."

I looked at my day, and it didn't feel like this giant empty pit I had to fill. It just felt like... a day.

What happened? I'm not totally sure. But I think I finally stopped trying to make retirement feel like work. I stopped comparing every day to when I had a job. And I stopped waiting to suddenly feel great about being retired.

I just started accepting that this was different. Not better than working. Not worse. Just different. Really different. And that was okay.

The Identity Experiments

Week Seven became my laboratory. Since I didn't know who I was anymore, I decided to try different versions of myself.

Monday, I was "Cheryl the Writer" and spent the morning writing my book. Tuesday, I became "Cheryl the Student" and watched instructional YouTube videos. Wednesday was "Cheryl the Sister" day, and I went to lunch with my sister. Thursday, "Cheryl the Creative" appeared, and I pulled out a knitting project I hadn't touched in decades.

Most of these experiments failed. But failure in retirement doesn't carry the same consequences as failure at work. There's no performance review, no disappointed boss, no missed targets. Failure in retirement is just information: "Okay, that's not who I am."

Day 50: The Unexpected Breakthrough

Day 50. I was doing the same thing I'd been doing every morning - lying there staring at the ceiling, thinking about all the ways I was going to waste another day.

But that morning felt different somehow. I don't know if I was just too tired to keep beating myself up about retirement, or if something finally clicked after seven weeks of this. Maybe both.

I realized I'd been treating retirement like a job I was failing at. Every morning I'd wake up thinking I had to 'accomplish retirement'—fill the hours productively, find my grand purpose, prove I wasn't wasting my life. It was exhausting. That morning, I asked myself a different question. Not 'What should I do today?' but 'What am I actually curious about?'

The answer surprised me. I was scrolling through Facebook when I saw someone making jackets from vintage quilts. Wait, what? How do you even do that? So, I went down a YouTube rabbit hole watching videos about it.

One sewist said something that stopped me cold: tons of fabric— clothes, home linens, all of it—ends up in landfills every year. But this? This was taking something that someone had loved and used and giving it new life so someone else could love and use it.

I kept researching. Watched more videos. Started thinking about all the vintage materials I had access to, all those buttons from my mother's collection. For the first time in fifty days, I'd followed something I was curious about. Not something I thought I should do—something I wanted to know about. And it felt like maybe, just maybe, I'd found something that mattered.

That probably sounds like nothing. But when you've spent 45 years with every single hour planned out, doing something just because you're curious about it? That felt huge.

I stopped trying to solve retirement like it was a work problem. I was just... living and noticing things. Following whatever seemed interesting. Day 50 felt different than the other days. It was less like I was forcing myself through it. Less desperate. Like maybe I'd figure this whole thing out eventually.

The Relationship Recalibration

By Week Eight, the real challenge appeared: my marriage. Ed was very involved with the state floral association as president, and our rhythms were entirely out of sync. I'd want to talk when he was in the middle of a planning session or writing the president's message for the monthly magazine. He needed to complete his work.

We had our first retirement fight on Day 53. Not about money or major decisions—about me reorganizing his home office while he was away on floral association business. In my endless free time, I'd decided to "help" by completely rearranging his space. He came home to find his carefully organized chaos transformed into my version of order.

"I can't find anything!" he said.

"I was trying to help," I protested.

"I don't need help. I need my space to stay in my space."

That's when I realized: retirement isn't just about finding your own new identity. It's about renegotiating every relationship in your life. The templates in Toolkit #4 at the end of this chapter have specific guidance for navigating these relationship changes without destroying them.

Time Got Weird

Around the second month, I couldn't figure out what was happening with time.

Mornings were brutal. I'd eat breakfast. Look at the clock. 9:30. Okay, it's still morning. I'd sit there. Watched the morning news. Look at the clock again. 9:45. Are you kidding me? It had been forever. That's what it felt like anyway.

But weeks? Weeks just vanished. I have no idea how. One day it was Monday, and I was thinking about what to do with my week. Next thing I know, it's Friday. What did I even do? I couldn't tell you.

Each hour crawled by. But the weeks flew. How does that even work?

It reminded me of being a kid stuck in a boring class. You're watching the clock, wanting it to move faster, and it just... doesn't. Except now there was no bell. No end of the day. Just more time stretching out in front of me with nothing to fill it.

Without meetings or deadlines, the days just blended together. I have no idea what I did on Tuesday in week six. Or Thursday. They were the same day as far as I could tell.

Coffee. Check the news. Eat lunch. Hit that afternoon wall around 2 PM. Make dinner. Watch TV. Go to bed. The next day, the same thing.

Everything felt the same. And that terrified me. Was this it? Was this going to be my life for the next twenty years? Just the same forgettable day over and over?

The Research Behind My Experience

Though I was wondering what was happening to me, it wasn't as weird as I thought. The National Bureau of Economic Research conducted a 2021 study on how retirees spend their time. Between days 30 and 60, they found something interesting — people's perception of time changes. Almost everyone reported the same thing: the days felt endless but also pointless. Time was crawling by, but none of it mattered.

That's precisely what happened to me. The hours would drag on forever, but at the end of the day, I couldn't point to anything that felt more worthwhile.

So, I started making up little rituals. Nothing big - I'd already tried big, and that didn't work. Just small stuff that made the days feel different from each other.

Monday became laundry day. Not because I had that much laundry. I just needed Monday to be something. On Wednesday, I'd have lunch with my sister. That became my thing to get to - like if I could make it to Wednesday lunch, I'd made it through half the week. On Saturday mornings, I'd browse thrift stores for vintage quilts. Most of the time, I didn't find any. But it gave me a reason to get up and leave the house.

These weren't exciting anchors. But they kept me from completely losing track of time, from looking up one day and realizing I couldn't remember what month it was. Without them, retirement would have been one long, shapeless Tuesday that lasted forever.

Day 60: The Assessment

Two months in, I finally started to understand myself without the structure of work imposing its rhythm on me. Turns out I'm a morning person—who knew? For forty-five years, I'd forced myself to be productive from 8 to 5 because that's what work demanded. But left to my own devices, I was sharp from 7 to 11 AM and basically worthless after lunch. Those afternoons I'd been trying to force productivity? My brain doesn't work like that. By evening, I wasn't fatigued. Just done. Ready to sit and read, knit, or zone out.

Here's what surprised me, though. I thought I'd miss being a director. The status of it. All those meetings back-to-back. The rush of putting out fires and fixing things fast.

I didn't miss any of that. Not even a little. What I missed was having a problem that mattered. Something where somebody needed me to figure it out.

Knowing that people were counting on me for something specific. The little hit of satisfaction when I could help someone figure something out.

And then there were the unexpected gifts of retirement. Grocery shopping at 10 AM on a Tuesday—the store is nearly empty, no rushed people with screaming kids, time to read labels. Sitting down with a book after breakfast and looking up to realize I'd read three hundred pages, and it was dinnertime. Best of all: that moment when someone asks what day it is and you honestly have no idea, and for the first time in your adult life, it doesn't matter.

Complete the Toolkit #4 and then continue to Chapter 6 to see how your life starts to settle in the last thirty days of your 90-day journey into your retirement.

<hr />

Toolkit #4
Days 31 - 60 Survival Templates

Week 5: The Novelty is Dead (Days 31-37)

Day 31: The Thud

Your Day 31 Reality Check:

- This feeling is universal—you're not broken
- Change one element of your routine
- Visit somewhere new
- Contact someone unexpectedly
- Wear something you never wore to work

Day 35: The Statistical Low Point

Research shows that Day 35 is when most retirees hit rock bottom.

Your Day 35 Emergency Protocol:

- DO NOT make any major decisions today
- Call your most understanding friend
- Exercise harder than usual
- Do something that helps someone else
- Remember: This is the bottom; it goes up from here

Day 37: Pushing Through

Your Push-Through Plan:

- One foot in front of the other
- One small meaningful action
- One connection with another human
- One thing to look forward to tomorrow
- One hour at a time if necessary

Week 6-7: Identity Experiments (Days 38-51)

Day 40: The Subtle Shift

Your Shift Indicators:

- Waking up without immediately calculating hours to fill
- One activity you actually look forward to
- Less guilt about "productivity"
- Occasional moments of peace
- Glimpses of who you might become

Day 45: Trying on New Identities

Your Identity Experiment Week:

- Monday: The Learner (take a class, watch documentaries)
- Tuesday: The Creator (make something, anything)
- Wednesday: The Helper (volunteer, help someone)
- Thursday: The Social One (connect with people)
- Friday: The Explorer (go somewhere new)

See what fits. Most won't. That's fine.

Day 49: Relationship Reality Check

Your Relationship Audit:

- Which work friendships are surviving?

  ____

- How is your primary relationship adjusting?

  ____

- Which family relationships are changing?

  ____

- Who new has entered your life?

  ____

- What relationship needs immediate attention?

Week 8: Approaching the Milestone (Days 52-60)

Day 55: Patterns Emerge

Your Pattern Recognition:

- When is your best energy? Schedule accordingly

- What brings satisfaction? Do more

- What consistently feels empty? Do less

- Which people energize you? See them more

- What structure works? Keep it

Day 60: Two Months Survived

Open that letter from Day 30. See how far you've come.

Your Two-Month Reality:

- The panic isn't as constant anymore
- Some routines feel normal now
- You've had a day or two that didn't feel pointless
- The "who am I" question isn't screaming quite as loud
- You can imagine this might work

That's progress. Real progress.

You're two-thirds through. The final month is about discovering your sustainable patterns.

The Research Behind My Experience

Month Two almost broke me. But it wasn't about me failing, something changes in your brain during this time.

The National Bureau of Economic Research found that between days 30 and 60, people's sense of time gets warped. The days drag on forever but feel completely pointless.

King's College London published research on how your brain adjusts to retirement. They found that your brain panics when you take away the structure of work. It doesn't know how to create a sense of purpose anymore. They call it "purpose void syndrome."

It takes your brain about 45 to 60 days to start building new pathways—new ways to feel like you accomplish something that doesn't depend on work.

If someone had told me this was temporary, that my brain needed 6 or 8 weeks to rewire, I might have panicked less.

CHAPTER 6

Days 61-90 - Stabilizing Your New Life

"The key to retirement is to find joy in the little things."
— Susan Miller

Day 61: The Settling

Somewhere in the third month—I think it was a Thursday, but I can't be sure—I woke up and didn't immediately calculate how many days I'd been retired. The mental ticker that had been running since April ('Day 23 of unemployment,' 'Day 47 of irrelevance') had finally gone quiet. I made coffee, watched the news, and got halfway through the morning before realizing I hadn't once thought about what I should be doing.

The change was so gradual, I'd missed it happening. The chest-tightening panic of Month One had faded to occasional unease. Instead of desperately trying to prove I was still productive, I'd started simply doing things that seemed worth doing, working on my craft projects when the mood struck—writing in my journal some mornings, skipping it on others without the guilt that would have crushed me six weeks earlier.

I was still lost. Let me be clear about that. I didn't have any grand purpose. No exciting second career. No inspiring comeback story.

But something did change around day 60. Being lost didn't feel like a crisis anymore. I was still wandering around with no real plan. But instead of panicking about it, I started getting curious.

Like, what if I tried this thing? What would happen? I didn't know where any of it was leading, but that was okay. I was noticing things I wouldn't have paid attention to if I'd had it all figured out.

Does that make sense? The "Oh God, what am I doing with my life" feeling shifted to more like "Huh, that's interesting, let me see where this goes."

I wasn't giving up. My body just finally believed this was real. This was my life now. So, it stopped treating every single day like an emergency.

The Routine Revolution

By week nine, I had a routine. Not the kind I tried to force in the beginning - those didn't work. This one sort of happened because I paid attention to what actually felt okay versus what made me miserable.

Mornings were for creation—writing, planning, and thinking. Afternoons for connection—lunch with friends, crafting, errands that involved human contact. Evenings for restoration—reading and being with Ed. I hadn't decided on this schedule; it had decided itself based on when I naturally had energy for different activities.

There's a difference between forcing yourself into a schedule and just figuring out what works. One feels like you're fighting yourself all day. The other... fits.

Week Ten: What Am I Even Doing Here

I stopped trying to find my Big Purpose. I was too tired to keep looking for some grand reason I was put on this earth. And you know what? When I stopped looking for one big thing, I found a few small things instead.

Making upcycled crafts, going to church choir rehearsal on Wednesday nights, and writing this book. None of these would change the world, but together they created a life of gentle significance.

I stopped asking "What is my purpose?" and started asking "What needs doing that I can do?" The first question paralyzed me. The second one mobilized me.

Day 75: The Social Reconfiguration

Two and a half months in, my social landscape had completely transformed. Work friends had faded to LinkedIn connections and occasional texts and phone calls. Some family relationships had intensified—my sister and I went from occasional texts to weekly lunches. New people appeared—fellow choir members, neighbors I'd never had time to know, women in the mahjong club.

But the most significant social change was with Ed. We'd been married for 48 years, but retirement brought us back together all over again. Without work stories to share, we had to find new topics to discuss. Without separate daily experiences, we had to create individual space within togetherness.

Ed was used to having the house to himself all day. He had his routines down to a science. Monday was his laundry day—except now I'd beat him to the washing machine. He'd be at the sink washing dishes when I'd squeeze in to get water for bread-making. After two months of stepping on each other's toes, Day 75 brought our breakthrough conversation:

'I need you to stop disrupting my routine,' Ed said.

'I'm just trying to get my stuff done,' I protested.

'But you're in my space when I'm washing dishes. Can't you wait?'

'I didn't realize I was bothering you. I just needed water for my bread.'

'I haven't been able to keep my daily schedule since you retired.'

That's when I realized - I hadn't just retired from my job. I'd moved into Ed's house. I mean, it's our house. But he'd been running it his way for years, and suddenly I was just... there. All the time. In his space.

We had to figure out some ground rules. I do laundry on Monday afternoons now - that's my time. I wait until he's done with the dishes before I start baking because otherwise, we're both in the kitchen tripping over each other. He tells me if he's got plans, so I'm not just sitting around wondering whether we're doing something together.

Is it perfect? No. But we're figuring it out.

The Research Behind My Experience

What surprised me in the 2021 University of Michigan Health and Retirement Study is that 68% of couples report significant stress in their relationship during the first 90 days of retirement. That is more than half. And what were they fighting over the most? Territory. In other words, who does what, who's in charge of which spaces, and whose routine takes priority.

The European Social Science & Aging Survey examined this in 2023 and became more specific about it. Couples who don't sit down and renegotiate their household territories within the first three months are three times more likely to report ongoing unhappiness in retirement. Three times. That's not a slight difference.

I wish I'd known this was coming. Maybe we could have had those conversations before we got to the point of snapping at each other over whose turn it was to wash clothes.

The Health Surprise

By Week Eleven, my body had finally adjusted to retirement. The 3 AM anxiety wakeups had stopped. The afternoon crashes disappeared. I was sleeping through the night for the first time in decades.

But I'd also gained eight pounds. I found I was eating more and moving less. The "retirement fifteen" is real, and I was on track to achieve it.

This forced another recalibration. Movement had to become intentional rather than incidental. Eating had to become conscious rather than recreational. The daily templates in Toolkit #5 helped me build healthy habits without the all-or-nothing mentality that sabotages so many retirement health plans.

Day 85: The Comparison Trap

Day 85, I made the mistake of visiting my sister. She's retired for over 15 years, and it shows. Her house looks like something from Better Homes and Gardens—every surface clear, every closet organized, those little labels on everything. I sat in her backyard with my coffee, surrounded by what can only be described as paradise. Rose bushes that actually bloom. A rock garden with no weeds. Perfectly trimmed Crepe Myrtles. Even her mulch looked perfect.

'I work out here every morning for a couple of hours,' she said, deadheading something that already looked flawless. 'It's my meditation.'

I nodded as I understood, but all I could think about was my own backyard with its single oak tree and the flower bed I'd been meaning to plant since 2018. For years, I'd told myself that retirement would be when I'd finally created my own garden paradise. I bought gardening books and even picked out which corner would get the roses. And here I was, nearly three months retired, and the only thing I'd planted was myself on the couch most afternoons.

Driving home, I felt like I was failing retirement. My sister had mastered this life; she had her gardens, her perfect routine, and she had everything organized. What did I have to show for three months? I couldn't even keep track of what day it was, much less keep a garden. I was still celebrating small victories like showering before noon.

But then I remembered something. Fifteen years ago, when my sister first retired, she was so burned out, and it took her over a year to recover and get back into the swing of things. Today, she says retirement at that time was probably not the smartest decision she made, but it was her favorite. That paradise in her backyard? It didn't spring up overnight. It took 15 years of mornings, 15 years of learning, 15 years of patience. I hadn't even started developing yet.

I was two and a half months into retirement. She'd been retired for fifteen years. Fifteen years. And I was comparing myself to her?

Of course, she had it figured out. She'd had over a decade to mess up and fix things. Try gardening and figure out what grows in Texas. Build a routine that worked for her.

Me? I was still trying to get through a Tuesday afternoon without losing my mind.

We weren't even in the same place. Not close.

Week Twelve: The Integration Begins

As Day 90 approached, something shifted. The old Cheryl (Director) and the new Cheryl (retired person, human being, still figuring it out) began to integrate. I wasn't replacing my old identity—I was expanding it.

I was still analytical, but now I analyzed how to lay patterns on upcycled fabric to get the most from each piece while minimizing waste. I was still strategic, but now the strategy was about filling my days with things that mattered, rather than planning successful quarters. I was still a leader, but I was leading my own life rather than a department.

The things I was good at in my career didn't just vanish. I still have those skills. They just work differently now.

I didn't have to pretend I'd never been a director. I didn't have to act like those 45 years didn't matter. I just had to figure out how to apply what I learned to the new life I'm building.

Day 90: The Assessment and the Acceptance

Day 90 fell on a Wednesday. I know because it was lunch day with my sister, and I mentioned the milestone. 'Three months already?' she said. 'Feels like yesterday you called me crying from your car.' It felt like yesterday and also like a lifetime ago.

I'd had such specific visions of who I'd be by now. Retirement Cheryl was supposed to be taking Spanish classes, maybe planning a cruise, definitely with a thriving garden and an organized house. She'd wake up grateful every morning for her freedom, never miss a day of work, and never doubt her decision. That woman never showed up.

Instead, I was someone I didn't quite recognize yet but was starting to find interesting. I still had days where I stood in my kitchen at 11 AM, wondering what the point was. But I also had days where I got so absorbed in sewing that I forgot to eat lunch. The desperate need to know who I was had softened into curiosity about who I might become.

What I worried about changed.

Early on, I'd wake up in a panic. "What am I supposed to do today? Who even am I anymore? How do I make any of this matter?"

Now, when I wake up, I still ask myself questions. Just different ones. "What sounds good today?" Sometimes it's "What have I been putting off that I should actually deal with?" Or "Does anyone need help with something?"

I wouldn't call it peace. That sounds too final, like I'd figured everything out. But that constant panic? Gone.

You know that awful feeling of falling without a parachute? Mine shifted to something more like floating. I didn't know where I was headed—no clue where I'd land. But at least I wasn't bracing for the crash anymore.

And that emptiness I'd been scrambling to fill? It started feeling less like a void and more like breathing room—space to think without meetings stacked on meetings, without deadlines, without someone evaluating my performance.

Three months. It wasn't enough time to build a new life, but it was enough to stop mourning the old one quite so much.

The Truth About Day 91

Everyone asks about Day 90 as if it's a finish line. As if after three months, you've officially transitioned and retirement has appropriately begun. The truth is, Day 91 looks a lot like Day 90, which looks a lot like Day 89.

The transition doesn't end at 90 days—it just becomes less urgent. The identity crisis doesn't resolve—it just becomes less of a crisis and more of an evolution. The purpose doesn't suddenly appear; it continues to appear in small, daily choices.

What does change by Day 90 is your relationship with uncertainty. You've survived three months of not knowing who you are, and you haven't died. You've faced the void of unstructured time, and it hasn't swallowed you. You've lost your professional identity, and you still exist.

That survival becomes confidence. Not confidence that you have retirement figured out—confidence that you can figure it out as you go.

The 90-day milestone isn't an ending. It's proof that you can do this. You can be without doing. You can matter without meetings. You can have purpose without a position.

You can be Cheryl—or whoever you are—without the title, without the office, without the external validation. Just you, living your days, creating meaning from the raw material of time and freedom.

That's not retirement success. That's human success. And it's enough.

Complete the Toolkit #5 **Days 61 - 90 Survival Templates** and then continue to Chapter 7 for guidance on navigating special challenges that may arise during your retirement journey. The 90 days are behind you, but the adventure continues.

Toolkit #5
Days 61 - 90 Survival Templates Crisis Management Tools & 90-Day Tracker

Week 9-10: Integration Begins (Days 61-74)

Day 61: Stop Counting Days

Switch to week-based thinking.

Your Week-Based Plan:

- Plan by week, not day
- Assess by month, not week
- One anchor activity per week
- One social commitment per week
- One growth activity per week

Day 70: Purpose Appears (Lowercase P)

Your Purpose Building Blocks:

- One way to help weekly
- One thing to learn monthly
- One problem to solve (tiny counts)
- One person to support
- One thing to create

<u>Week 11-12: Approaching Graduation (Days 75-90)</u>

Day 75: Relationship Stabilization

Your Relationship Reality:

- New boundaries with spouse established
- Real friends separated from work proximity friends
- New connections beginning to form
- Family dynamics adjusted
- Support system identified

Day 85: Confidence Emerging

Your Confidence Markers:

- Whole days without retirement panic
- Genuine enjoyment of some activities
- Less comparison to working life
- Acceptance of the uncertainty
- Hope for what's ahead

Day 90: Graduation Day

Your 90-Day Assessment:

You survived:

- Your entire identity getting ripped away
- Days of feeling useless and empty
- Being bored out of your mind
- Relationships getting weird
- 3 AM money panic
- Not knowing what comes next

What you've built:

- Some routines that work
- Your emergency plan for bad days

- A couple of people you can talk to
- A few things that might matter
- Evidence that you're more adaptable than you thought

You made it 90 days. That's something.

Emergency Day Templates

The Panic Day Template
    When anxiety is overwhelming:
    7 AM: Acknowledge the panic
    8 AM: Exercise (force yourself)
    9 AM: Shower, dress properly
    10 AM: Leave the house immediately
    11 AM: Human contact (anywhere)
    12 PM: Eat actual food
    1 PM: Call a supportive person
    2 PM: Simple project
    3 PM: Walk again
    4 PM: Early dinner prep
    5 PM: No news allowed
    6 PM: Comfort activity
    8 PM: Early bed

The Depression Day Template

When you can't get motivated:
    Start whenever: One small win
    Then: Shower (counts as second win)
    Then: Dress in real clothes
    Then: One nutritious thing
    Then: 10 minutes outside
    Then: One text to someone
    Then: One page of reading
    Then: One creative act (tiny)

Then: Acknowledge you tried
Then: Tomorrow will be different

The Rage Day Template

When you're angry at everything:
    Morning: Journal the rage out
    Then: Hard physical exercise
    Then: Break something safely (ice, twigs)
    Then: Call someone who gets it
    Then: Do the opposite action (help someone)
    Then: Create something
    Then: Watch comedy
    Then: Early bed
    Tomorrow: Fresh start

The Numb Day Template

When you feel nothing:
    Any time: Change physical position
    Then: Change physical location
    Then: Change temperature (hot shower/cold air)
    Then: Strong sensation (spicy food, loud music)
    Then: Human contact
    Then: Physical movement
    Then: One decision (any decision)
    Then: One emotion (any emotion)
    Then: Acknowledge the numbness will pass

Your Personal 90-Day Tracking

Week 1 ☐ Survived

Hardest part: ____
Best moment: ____

Week 2 □ Survived

Hardest part: ____

Best moment: ____

Week 3 □ Survived

Hardest part: ____

Best moment: ____

Week 4 □ Survived

Hardest part: ____

Best moment: ____

Month 1 □ Complete

Week 5 □ Survived

Hardest part: ____

Best moment: ____

Week 6 □ Survived

Hardest part: ____

Best moment: ____

Week 7 □ Survived

Hardest part: ____

Best moment: ____

Week 8 □ Survived

Hardest part: ____

Best moment: ____

Month 2 □ Complete

Week 9 ☐ Survived

Hardest part: ____
Best moment: ____

Week 10 ☐ Survived

Hardest part: ____
Best moment: ____

Week 11 ☐ Survived

Hardest part: ____
Best moment: ____

Week 12 ☐ Survived

Hardest part: ____
Best moment: ____

Month 3 ☐ Complete

90 Days ☐ Survived

The Bottom Line

The first 90 days aren't about building your extraordinary retirement life. They're about surviving the transition. If you're reading this thinking, "I'm failing at retirement," you're not. You're right on schedule. The confusion, boredom, panic, and identity crisis aren't signs of failure—they're signs of transition.

Your only job in the first 90 days is to survive them. If you're vertical and breathing on Day 91, you've succeeded.

———— • ————

CHAPTER 7

Special Retirement Transition Challenges

"Don't simply retire from something; have something to retire to."
— Harry Emerson Fosdick

When Retirement Chooses You

You don't always get to choose when you retire. About 40% of us retire earlier than we planned - health problems, layoffs, needing to take care of family. I'm in that 40%.

When retirement is forced on you, it's not just the financial disruption that hurts—it's the emotional whiplash. You didn't get to say goodbye on your terms. Maybe you still had goals to achieve, people you loved working with, projects you wanted to complete. Losing that feels like grief because that's precisely what it is.

If this is your story too, know this: you're allowed to be angry. You're allowed to feel cheated. You're allowed to mourn the retirement party you didn't get, the gradual transition you'd planned, and the final year you thought you'd have.

What helped me move through it: permitting myself to feel everything first, then slowly reconstructing my narrative. Instead of "I was laid off," I began saying "I retired earlier than planned." Instead of "I had no choice," I shifted to "The timing was chosen for me, but what I do now is my choice."

The story you tell yourself about your retirement shapes your experience of it.

The Research Behind My Experience

Getting laid off at 69 was terrible. But at least I'm not alone in this.

The Urban Institute conducted research showing that 37% of retirees are forced out earlier than they planned, more than a third. We're not outliers - we're a huge group. And if you're over 65 like I was, there's another problem. If you think about going back to work, you're facing age discrimination on top of everything else.

The Transamerica Institute published a 2023 report on retirement transitions. They looked specifically at people like me who didn't choose to retire. What they found is we're dealing with what could be considered a double adjustment burden. You're grieving that you didn't get to choose, and at the same time, you're trying to figure out how to be retired—two complicated things at once.

The numbers from their research were sobering. People in our situation are 50% more likely to be depressed in the first year. Fifty percent. And it takes us about eight months longer than voluntary retirees to say we're satisfied with our lives.

Eight months. That's a long time to be struggling.

If you're reading this because you were pushed into retirement, as I was, I want you to know something. What you're going through is real. It's harder than voluntary retirement - the research proves that. But here's the other thing the research shows: it's surmountable. People get through it. I'm getting through it. You can too.

The High Achiever's Dilemma

For 45 years, I knew exactly how well I was doing. I turned in reports early. I always met or exceeded every quota. I got promoted ahead of schedule. There were numbers, reviews, raises, titles—all these ways to measure whether I was succeeding or failing.

In retirement? There's nothing. No metrics. No performance reviews. Just you, trying to figure out if you're doing this right, whatever "this" even means. And comparing yourself to your sister's perfect garden doesn't count—that's a competition you'll lose every time.

Without any way to measure if I was doing okay, my brain just lost it. Was I good at being retired? Bad at it? How was I supposed to know? Nobody gives you a performance review for retirement. Nobody tells you, "Hey, good job making it through Tuesday."

So, I made a spreadsheet. I know. In week three, I sat down and made a spreadsheet to track what I did each day. Took a shower before 9 AM - I'd mark it down. Made the bed - check. Left the house for something - check.

I even bought gold star stickers. Put them on a chart like I was five years old.

It was ridiculous. But I needed something. Some way to feel like I'd done something, accomplished anything at all.

I talked to someone else who retired around the same time as I did. She tried to fill every single day. She took classes, signed up for committees, and volunteered for three different things. She was busier retired than when she was working. Then she crashed. Just completely burned out from trying to stay busy enough to feel like she mattered.

The shift happened slowly for me. I don't remember exactly when. But I was working on something with my sister for our craft business - we were trying to figure out the right way to explain what we do, why we use our mother's old buttons in the pieces we make. And it clicked. We got it right. Nobody was going to give me an award for that. It wasn't going on any resume. But it felt good, in a way, in a way my work accomplishments never really did. It mattered because it mattered to us. Not because someone was measuring it.

That's when I started to understand. Achievement in retirement isn't about climbing higher. It's about going deeper. Deeper into conversations, deeper into relationships, deeper into the things you glossed over while racing to the next promotion. My brain still struggles to recognize these quieter victories as 'achievements,' but it's learning. Slowly.

The Workaholic's Withdrawal

If you're someone who lived for work—and I absolutely was—retirement hits you like a truck. Your body doesn't know what to do with itself. Your brain keeps looking for the next thing to fix, the next problem to solve.

I'd check my email 20 times a day, even though no work emails were coming in. I'd wake up at 5:45 AM, ready to start a commute that didn't exist anymore. I'd feel guilty watching TV at 2 PM, like someone might walk in and catch me not working. It was ridiculous. But I couldn't stop.

Recovering from workaholism in retirement involves a similar approach to recovering from any addiction.

- Acknowledge that you have an addiction (work gave you a high)
- Find what triggers it (boredom, feeling useless)
- Find something healthy to replace it (volunteer work, hobbies with deadlines)
- Be patient if you relapse (you might take on too much too soon)
- Get help and support (from other recovering workaholics, aka retirees)

The "Who Needs Who" Crisis

For 45 years, people needed me. My team needed me to sign off on things. Other departments needed my input. People came to me with problems because I knew how things worked, the history, and what had been tried before.

Then I retired. And nobody needed me for anything anymore.

All that stuff I knew? All those years of experience? It didn't matter. Nobody wanted it. Nobody was asking for it. I'd spent decades learning this job, getting good at it, and now it was... useless information taking up space in my head.

The crisis isn't about being needed; it's about mattering, which in retirement requires intention. You must proactively find opportunities to create value, rather than wait for responsibilities to be assigned to you.

I found that I matter in unexpected places:

I matter at the church where I sing in the choir

I matter to my sister's plants when she travels

I matter to my grandchildren, who think my terrible jokes are hilarious

It's not the same as being needed at work, but it's a real need. A need that really matters. You have to look for it rather than have it delivered to your inbox.

The Couple's Collision

If you're married or in a partnership, retirement doesn't just affect you. My retirement completely disrupted Ed's life, and he wasn't even the one retiring.

When Ed retired, he took on the household laundry (towels, sheets, kitchen towels, etc.), kitchen duties, and grocery shopping. As the president of the state floral association, he was often on the phone or on conference calls. He had his own way of doing things. Then I entered his perfectly functioning household like a hurricane, rearranging things, expressing my opinions about laundry timing, and getting in his way in the kitchen when he was trying to clean up. I had become the invader in what had been his domain for years.

We went from seeing each other for a few hours a day to being together all day, every day. It was like moving in together all over again, except we had been married for 48 years and had our own fixed ways of doing things.

It took us six months to figure out a solution. We had already chosen separate spaces; Ed has an office, and I have my craft and office space upstairs. We scheduled time apart, which turned out to be just as important as our time together. Instead of assuming what we needed, we actually communicated—what a novel idea! Most importantly, we had to be patient with each other during this adjustment period. This was the most significant change we made because of my retirement.

The Health Scare Wake-Up

Here's what I didn't expect - retirement didn't make me healthier. I thought I'd feel better without all the work stress. But my body got weird in ways I wasn't ready for.

I'd been running on work stress since 1979. That's a long time. My body was used to it. And then suddenly it was just... gone. No more adrenaline. No more constant low-level panic about deadlines and meetings.

My stress headaches went away, which was great. But then other things started hurting. My back. My neck. Places that never bothered me before. My stomach was a mess. For decades, I'd lived on coffee and sandwiches eaten at my desk in ten minutes. Now I was sitting down to actual meals, and my digestion didn't know what to do with that.

And the anxiety was worse. Which makes no sense, right? I wasn't stressed about work anymore. But my body didn't get the memo. It was like my system was so used to being stressed that when there was nothing actually to be stressed about, it just made up reasons to panic.

You may experience various changes in your health after retirement. Stress-related issues may either improve or uncover underlying problems. Sleep patterns will change significantly, and energy levels may fluctuate. Appetite and weight often shift as well. During this time, it's essential to pay attention to your mental health needs.

Health recalibration can take months. Eight months in, I'm still figuring out this new body I'm living in.

The Geography Question

Should you move? Downsize? Relocate to be near grandchildren? Move to that beach town you've always dreamed about?

Everyone has opinions about how you should approach your retirement geography. But here's what I learned: don't make any significant geographic changes in your first year of retirement. You're already adjusting to the most important life change imaginable. Adding a geographic change multiplies the stress exponentially.

If you must move (for financial or health reasons), recognize that you're really managing two major transitions. Be extra patient with yourself. Build support systems before you need them. And know that it will take longer to feel settled—both in retirement and in your new location.

The Money Reality Check

Even with sound financial planning, the psychological shift from earning to spending is jarring. That first month when money only goes out, nothing comes in—except maybe Social Security or retirement accounts—feels wrong at a cellular level.

I'd check our bank balance obsessively; sure, we were hemorrhaging money even though we were well within budget. The guilt about spending on "non-essentials" was crushing. Who was I to buy anything new when I wasn't earning?

It took months to internalize that this is what we'd saved for. The money was there to be used, not hoarded out of fear. But that psychological shift from accumulation to distribution is harder than any financial advisor warned me about.

Moving Forward When the Path Isn't Clear

Every retirement challenge feels unique when you're in it, but know this: whatever you're struggling with, thousands of retirees have faced it before. You're not weak at finding it hard. You're not failing for feeling lost. You're not broken for grieving your old life even when you chose to leave it.

The special challenges of retirement are special because they're yours. Your specific combination of circumstances, personality, history, and hopes creates a unique retirement puzzle. But puzzles are meant to be solved, piece by piece, with patience and persistence.

Some days you'll force pieces that don't fit. Some days you'll want to sweep the whole puzzle off the table. But gradually, the picture appears. Your retirement picture. Unlike anything you imagined while working, but yours, nonetheless.

CHAPTER 8

Building Your Retirement Support Team

*"Call it a clan, call it a network, call it a tribe, call it a family.
Whatever you call it, whoever you are, you need one."*
— Jane Howard

The Myth of Solo Retirement

I thought retirement would be my individual journey. My transition. My time. What I discovered: retirement is actually a team sport, and trying to play it alone is a recipe for misery.

The support team you need in retirement is different from your work network. It's not about professional advancement or strategic connections. It's about survival, sanity, and shared humanity. And unlike your work network, which is often formed naturally, your retirement support team requires intentional construction.

The Research Behind My Experience

When I insist you need a retirement support team, I'm not being dramatic—I'm being scientific. Harvard's Study of Adult Development, following subjects for over 80 years, found that relationship quality in retirement is the single strongest predictor of happiness and health—stronger than money, genetics, or career achievement.

The National Academy of Sciences' 2020 report was even more stark: social isolation in retirement increases health risks equivalent to smoking 15 cigarettes a day.

The Gerontological Society conducted a 2023 study titled "Aging Solo." They looked at retirees who lived alone or felt isolated. What they found was that if you have at least three people you connect with regularly - not just occasionally, but regularly - you're 40% less likely to get depressed.

My sister was a lifesaver for me. Those Wednesday lunches kept me sane. But one person isn't enough. You need more than that. The research backs that up.

The Inner Circle: Your Primary Support

Your Partner (If You Have One)

Ed became the most important person in all of this. But it didn't just happen automatically. We had to figure out how to be retired together.

For years, we'd been living sort of parallel lives. He was home, I was working. We had dinner together, we spent weekends together, but we had our own space during the day. Then suddenly, I was home all the time too. We were both just... there. All day. Every day.

We had to have conversations we'd never had before. Like, how much time together is good and how much is too much? I didn't know. He didn't know. We had to figure it out.

What did each of us want retirement to look like? I'd never asked him that. He'd never asked me. We just assumed we'd figure it out.

And the energy thing - some days I wanted to do something, and he wanted to stay home. Some days it was the opposite. We had to learn how to manage that without one of us always giving in and getting resentful.

Who does grocery shopping now? Who cooks? Who cleans? All that stuff we'd figured out for years suddenly needed renegotiating because I wasn't at work anymore.

The hardest part was figuring out how to be our own people when we're together all the time. I'm still me. He's still him. But when you're in the same house all day, every day, that gets blurry.

Here's what I learned - couples who do okay with this aren't the ones who never struggle. Everyone struggles. The ones who make it are the ones who actually talk about it instead of just being mad at each other.

Family Members Who Get It

Not everyone in your family will get it. My sister was a lifesaver - those Wednesday lunches became the thing I looked forward to every week. But other people? They might not understand at all.

You might have relatives who say things like "It must be so nice to be on vacation all the time!" Like retirement is just one long beach trip. Or they'll look at you like something's wrong with you because you're not thrilled every single day.

The worst is when people ask, "So what do you DO all day?" Not in a curious way. In that judgy way. Like they're implying you're just sitting around doing nothing. You try to explain, and it comes out sounding defensive or pathetic even to your own ears.

My sister never did that. She'd ask how I was doing and listen to the answer. When I'd tell her about a bad week, she wouldn't immediately try to fix it or tell me I should just be grateful. She'd say, "That sounds really hard."

That's what you need. People who understand this is a big deal. Who don't act like you're being dramatic when you say it's difficult. Who can listen without jumping in with advice or judgment.

And people who let you figure it out your own way instead of telling you what you should be doing with your retirement. Because everyone has opinions about what you should be doing, and most of them aren't helpful.

The Guides: People Who've Been There

Recent Retirees

You know who really helped me? Not people who'd been retired for ten years. They'd say things like "Oh, you'll love it eventually!" and I wanted to throw something at them.

The people who helped were the ones who'd retired maybe six months before me. A year at most. They still remembered how bad it was. They knew about waking up at 3 AM in a panic. They knew about those Tuesday afternoons when you want to cry for no reason.

But they were far enough along that they could tell me it gets better. And I believed them because they weren't that far ahead of me.

I met a few people like this - at church, through friends, just random conversations. And they'd say things like, "Yeah, in the second month I almost lost it," or "Wait till you hit about two and a half months, something shifts around then." They remembered the specific difficult parts. Not in a vague "Oh, it was tough" way. They remembered which days nearly broke them.

That's what I needed. Not someone telling me retirement is great. Someone telling me, "I felt like that too, and I'm okay now." Someone close enough to where I was that I could believe them.

Seasoned Retirees

People who'd been retired five or more years offered different wisdom—the long view. They'd forgotten the daily struggle of early retirement, but they could tell me what really mattered in the end versus what just felt urgent in the moment. They're proof that retirement life does stabilize, that you do find rhythm, that purpose does appear.

But be selective. Some long-term retirees had gotten stuck, bitter about forced retirement or isolated in their homes. I gravitated toward the ones who seemed engaged, who were still learning things, who could talk about their lives without mentioning their former careers every five minutes—the ones who'd become more themselves, not less.

The Professional Support

Financial Advisor

Even though the spreadsheets said we could afford retirement, I needed reassurance from our financial advisor. Not because the numbers changed—they didn't. But because my brain couldn't accept that we were okay. Every bill that came in triggered the thought: 'We're not earning anymore. We're just spending it down.'

Our advisor, bless her patience, understood this wasn't about math. It was about psychology. The shift from accumulation to spending goes against every instinct you've developed over 45 years. She didn't just manage our money; she helped with my anxiety. 'Cheryl,' she'd say, 'you saved for this exact purpose. The money is doing what it's supposed to do.'

Find an advisor who gets the emotional side, not just the numerical side. The best ones know that retirement money fears aren't rational, they're primal. You need someone who can address both the spreadsheet and the 3 AM panic that it's wrong.

Therapist or Counselor

I didn't use a therapist for my retirement transition, though I've used counseling at other times in my life and know its value. For me, my sister became my unofficial therapist, fielding daily crisis calls with the patience of a saint. Her many years of retirement wisdom and the ability to listen to me spiral without judgment saved my sanity. She normalized what I was experiencing and helped me see patterns I couldn't see on my own.

Not everyone has a sister they can call. I get that. If you don't have someone like that - someone who'll listen without judging - you might want to talk to a therapist.

I know. That sounds dramatic. But retirement messes with your head in ways I didn't expect. It's not like switching jobs or moving to a new house. It's more like losing someone or getting divorced. It's that level of upheaval, and nobody talks about it that way.

I've watched people struggle through this alone when they didn't have to. A few sessions with someone who understands life transitions - not regular therapy necessarily, just someone who gets what a big deal this is - could have saved them months of feeling lost.

I didn't do it. But if you're really struggling and you don't have people who understand, consider it. It's not a sign you're failing at retirement. It's just getting help with something that's hard.

Having used therapy at other life crossroads, I can tell you this: getting professional support during a crisis isn't weakness—it's wisdom. Whether it's a therapist, counselor, life coach, or, in my case, a patient sister, you need someone who can help you process what's happening without trying to fix you or minimize your experience.

Healthcare Team

Retirement changes your health needs. You have time for preventive care you skipped while working. You might need different medications as stress levels change. You certainly need providers who understand the challenges of retirement health.

Build your healthcare team before you need them urgently. Interview doctors while you're healthy. Establish relationships when you're not in crisis.

The Activity Partners

Exercise Buddy

Without the forced movement of work life, exercise must become intentional. But solo exercise in retirement can feel pointless. An exercise partner provides accountability, social connection, and structure.

My husband Ed became my exercise buddy. We walk together daily, and sometimes we pull out our bicycles for longer adventures. Having him as my built-in partner means I can't make excuses—he's right there, ready to go. It's time for us to talk without distractions, notice the changes in the neighborhood, and support our health together.

Learning Companions

Learning in retirement is nothing like professional development. There's no promotion waiting, no performance review to ace, no salary bump for mastering new skills. You're learning purely for the joy of it, which sounds lovely but can feel pointless when you're used to learning for advancement.

I'm planning to join a book club after the holidays, but in the meantime, I've found unexpected learning in places I didn't expect. Church choir has me tackling new music every week—sight-reading at 69 is humbling but exhilarating. The mahjong club I joined? I'm terrible at it, but my brain loves wrestling with the tiles and strategies. These aren't formal classes—they're joyful challenges that happen to come with built-in companions.

The key is finding learning that comes with people. Online courses are fine, but learning alone in retirement can deepen the isolation. When I'm struggling through a new choir piece with five other people who are also struggling, we're connected. When the mahjong ladies patiently explain the same rule for the third time, that's relationship-building disguised as game-playing.

Creative Collaborators

I've had this craft room for my knitting and sewing. But once I had time to use it, I realized that sitting there alone, making stuff, would've been depressing.

So, my sister and I decided to start doing craft fairs again. We had done one several years ago and stopped because life got too busy. Now we're back at it.

We'll sit down and throw ideas around - what should we make for the December fair? What actually sells versus what we think is cute? How do we make enough of something without spending three weeks on it? Then we just make things. Together. That's the part that matters.

Creating with my sister—bouncing ideas, solving problems, sharing the 'that won't work' moments, and the 'that's perfect' victories—gives purpose to what could have been solitary puttering. Even when we're working on different pieces, we're working toward the same goal.

The Purpose Partners

Volunteer Colleagues

What I missed most about work wasn't the actual work—it was the automatic colleagues. People you see regularly, work toward common goals with, and share inside jokes with. Volunteering gave that back, but better. No performance reviews, no politics, no competition, just people showing up to do something worthwhile together.

My church choir volunteers became my new work friends. We have our regular 'meetings' (rehearsals), our 'projects' (Sunday services), and our 'deadlines' (Easter cantata). But unlike work, when someone misses a note or comes in two beats late, we laugh instead of getting stressed. We're united by purpose without the poison of workplace dynamics.

Choose volunteer opportunities partly for the mission, sure, but mainly for the people. The right volunteer colleagues can replace what you miss about work relationships without any of what you don't miss.

Project Partners

This book almost didn't happen. I had forty thousand words of rambling retirement thoughts in various notebooks, computer files, and phone notes. It was overwhelming—like having all the ingredients for a cake spread across your kitchen with no recipe. I knew there was something there, but I couldn't shape it alone.

Finding someone to help me organize these thoughts changed everything. We met weekly, talking through my experiences while she asked questions that helped me dig deeper. The experiences are all mine, every panic attack, every small victory, every hard lesson learned—but having someone to help me shape them into chapters made the difference between having retirement stories and having a retirement book.

Retirement projects feel less overwhelming with partners. Whether it's writing a book, starting a business, or organizing the church rummage sale, having someone else invested in the outcome keeps you accountable and makes the work feel less lonely.

Building Your Team: Practical Steps

Building a support team sounds like some big formal thing. It's not. It's just paying attention to the people in your life and being honest about who really helps and who makes things worse.

Month 1: Assessment

In the first month, sit down and think about the people you actually talk to, your friends, your family, whoever. Then ask yourself some questions about each of them.

Who makes you feel better after you talk to them? And who makes you feel worse? Who gets what you're going through with this retirement thing? And who makes you feel like there's something wrong with you for struggling with it?

Be honest. Some people drain you. They do. Maybe they're negative all the time, maybe they judge you, perhaps they don't understand why you're not thrilled to be retired. Those people? You need to start pulling back from them. Not in a dramatic way. Just... less.

And the people who make you feel okay? The ones who listen, who don't judge, who maybe get what you're dealing with? Move toward them more. Call them more often. Make plans with them.

It sounds calculating when I put it like that. But you don't have extra energy right now to waste on people who make you feel bad.

Month 2: Try Everything

In the second month, you need to get out there and try stuff. Not to find your passion or commit to anything. Just to see what's out there and who you might meet.

Go to a library program. Try a class at the gym. Show up to a volunteer orientation. Whatever. The point isn't to sign up for everything. The point is to show up once and see what it's like.

Pay attention while you're there. Do you click with anyone? Does the conversation feel easy or forced? When you leave, do you feel energized or do you feel like you need a nap?

Your gut knows. When you meet your people, something feels right. You can't really explain it, but you know. Listen to that feeling.

Month 3: Investment

Choose 2-3 connections to deepen—regular coffee dates, walking meetings, shared activities. Building retirement friendships requires intention—you have to schedule them, nurture them, and show up even when you don't feel like it. Work forced regular contact. Retirement requires you to create it.

The maintenance never stops. Without work-forcing proximity, relationships fade fast. The weekly lunches, the regular volunteer shifts, the standing coffee dates, they're not just social activities. They're the infrastructure of retirement relationships.

Ongoing: Maintenance

Here's the thing about retirement friendships - they don't just happen on their own. At work, you saw people whether you wanted to or not—meetings, lunch breaks, whatever. The structure forced you to stay connected.

Now? You have to make it happen yourself. And if you don't, weeks go by, and you realize you haven't talked to anyone.

So, you need something regular. Wednesday lunch with your sister. A book club that meets on the first Thursday of every month. A volunteer shift you do every Tuesday. Whatever it is, put it on the calendar and then do it.

It's the regular part that matters. Not just "let's get together sometime." That never happens. It needs to be a specific day and time, something you can count on.

Otherwise, you drift apart without meaning to. I've seen it happen. People who were close... stop talking because neither of them picks up the phone.

The Support You Don't Need

Not everyone who offers support is helpful.

The people to avoid: Anyone who minimizes your struggle with 'At least you have money' or 'You should be grateful.' People who project their retirement dreams onto your reality. Anyone who makes you feel guilty for finding it hard. People stuck in their own difficult transitions who want company in their misery. The fixers who wish to manage your retirement for you, sending job listings because 'you seem bored.'

The support you need should support—not direct, not judge, not fix. The best support I got was from people who said, 'This is hard' without adding 'but.' They let me struggle without trying to solve me. They shared their own difficulties without comparing them to mine. They understood that validation was more helpful than advice.

The Surprising Truth

Building a support team in retirement felt like starting from scratch. Because that's basically what it was.

But here's what I didn't expect: starting over at 69 is different from starting over at 25. You're pickier. You know what you can't deal with anymore.

You don't have to be friends with people just because you collaborate with them. You don't have to stay connected to people who drain you just because you've known them for twenty years. You don't have to pretend to like someone you don't like.

That sounds harsh. But it's also kind of freeing. You get to choose now. Really choose. Not based on who's in your department or who lives on your street or who you're supposed to stay friends with, just based on who you want to spend time with.

Your retirement support team is curated, intentional, and genuine. These are people you choose and who choose you, without professional necessity binding you. That makes these relationships both more fragile and more real than work relationships ever were.

Six months into retirement, I realized something profound: I had fewer relationships but deeper ones: less quantity, more quality. And for the first time in decades, I had friends, real friends—not just colleagues pretending to be friends.

That might be retirement's greatest gift: the opportunity to build a support team based on who you are, not who you need to be for work. It takes effort, intention, and vulnerability. But the team you build becomes the foundation for everything good that follows.

Chapter 9 takes you beyond the 90-day transition to explore building your new life with intention and joy. Your support team will be crucial for that journey.

CHAPTER 9

Beyond Day 90 - Your New Beginning: Embracing the Journey Ahead

"Retirement: It's nice to get out of the rat race,
but you have to learn to get along with less cheese."
— Gene Perret

After the Transition

Day 91 was just another day. No big moment. No feeling of "I made it." Just a Thursday.

I realized at some point that week that I'd stopped counting days. Somewhere along the way, I stopped thinking of myself as "newly retired" and just started being... retired.

The first 90 days were about survival. Get through today without falling apart. Find a reason to get out of bed. Now I'm trying to actually build something. It's not the retirement I thought I'd have. It's not what other people believe retirement should look like. It's just whatever works for me.

Around Day 100, I stopped trying to solve retirement and started living it.

Finding Purpose (Or Purposes)

The first month, I was obsessed with finding my Purpose. Capital P. Something big to replace being a director. Something impressive to tell people.

I thought about consulting. Maybe start a business. But they felt wrong—either too much like having a job again or pointless.

It took me a while to realize I was looking for the wrong thing. I didn't need one big Purpose. I needed a bunch of smaller things that mattered.

Writing this book—someone out there is struggling and needs to know they're not crazy. Singing in the choir on Sundays. Being around for my family in ways I never could when I was working all the time, and being present instead of half-listening while thinking about work.

None of that sounds impressive if someone asks what I do now. "I sing in the church choir" doesn't have the same ring as "I'm a director at..."

But I don't care anymore. Or I'm learning not to care. Retirement purpose isn't about impressing people. It's about your Tuesday mattering to someone, about making something a tiny bit better just by showing up.

Figuring Out Your Days

Around month four, I started to understand something. There's a difference between just filling up time and doing things you really want to do.

Filling time was what I did at the beginning. Scroll through Netflix for three hours. Look through knitting patterns for the third time. Take a nap because I couldn't think of what else to do.

Then I started doing things because I wanted to. Not because they killed time. Because they sounded interesting.

I gave my days a loose theme. Not a schedule, I tried that, and it made me feel like I was at work again. Just a general idea. On Mondays, I'd think about the week ahead. Tuesdays, I'd move more—go for a walk, mess around in the house. Wednesday was lunch with my sister and choir practice. On Thursdays, I'd try learning something, like our mahjong club. Fridays felt like creative days.

It wasn't rigid. Some weeks it didn't work at all. But having a loose plan meant I was never standing in my kitchen at noon, wondering what to do with myself.

The difference between retirement that feels empty and retirement that feels full isn't about being busy. It's about choosing what fills your days, rather than desperately grabbing at anything to make time pass.

The Creativity Explosion

Around Month Five, my brain started creating again. Not just crafts—though my craft room finally got used. But creative problem-solving, creative life design, creative ways of being in the world.

I finished a blanket I'd started knitting three years ago. I'm writing this book. I tried making artisan bread—every loaf looks terrible, like someone sat on it, but they taste pretty good.

My sister and I are doing craft fairs again. We make hand-knit pillows and quilted Christmas ornaments from upcycled fabric. A lot of what we make has our mother's old buttons on it. She collected them for years. When she died, we inherited this vast collection. So now we put them on the things we make. It feels like a way to keep part of her with us.

At work, my brain was always full of deadlines, meetings, and whatever crisis was happening. There was no room for anything else. Now there is. I can think "what if I tried this?" and then try it. I can start a project and quit halfway through if it's not working. Nobody cares.

That's the weird part about retirement creativity. It's messy. I start things I don't finish. I make stuff that doesn't turn out right. But it doesn't matter if it's good or not. I'm just making it.

The Six-Month Revelation

About six months in, I went a whole week without thinking about work. At all. I saw something on LinkedIn from someone I used to work with and felt nothing. Work had been my whole life for 45 years. And now I could go for days without even remembering it existed.

That's when I started to figure something out. I thought I missed being a director— the title and status. But what I really missed was feeling useful and having structure, knowing what I was doing at 10 AM on a Tuesday.

Here's what surprised me: I didn't miss the recognition as much as I thought I would. What got to me was feeling stuck. At work, even when it was hard, I was always learning something new. Now I wasn't getting better at anything. I was just here, doing the same things every day.

Once I figured out what I missed versus what I thought I was supposed to miss, things got easier. I could find ways to feel useful without a job title. I could create structure without having a boss. I could learn new things without climbing some corporate ladder.

But that still left one nagging question.

The Legacy Question

Six months in, the legacy question hit me hard. What had forty-five years of work actually meant? Would anyone remember my contributions six months after I left? Probably not. The company moved on without missing a beat.

But then I started thinking about legacy differently. Legacy isn't what you left behind at work—that gets overwritten, updated, replaced. Legacy is what you're creating now.

I'm writing this book because maybe it'll help someone feel less crazy. I'm more available for my grandchildren—actually available, not just there while thinking about work. My sister and I are making crafts using our mother's buttons and upcycled fabric, keeping her memory alive.

None of this is as impressive as what I did at work. It won't go on a resume. But it's real. It's mine. And nobody can take it away from me with one phone call.

Making Your Own Rules

Around month seven, I wrote down some rules for myself. Not goals exactly. Just things I needed to remind myself of. The list is taped to my bathroom mirror, so I see it every morning.

Here's what I wrote:
- I'm not going to apologize for being retired.
- I'm not going to make myself busy to prove I'm not wasting my life.
- I need structure, but not so much that it feels like a prison.
- I'm keeping the friendships that make me feel good. The ones that drain me? I'm done with those.
- I'm not comparing my retirement to anyone else's. Not even my sister's.
- I can try new things without being good at them.
- I can ask for help without feeling pathetic.
- I can say no without giving a huge explanation.
- Small things count. Like getting dressed before noon. That's a win some days.
- I get to decide what success looks like for me.

Your list will be different. But write one. Put it somewhere you'll see it. When retirement feels overwhelming, read it. It helps.

The Financial Peace

The money anxiety didn't disappear overnight. For six months, every credit card bill triggered the thought: "We're not earning anymore." Every unexpected expense—roof repair, sprinkler system, property tax increase—sent me spiraling. I'd wake up at 3 AM doing math, even though we'd done the math a hundred times before retiring.

What finally calmed me was evidence. Month after month, the budget worked. We weren't hemorrhaging money. By Month Seven, I could pay bills without my chest tightening.

We check the budget every month. Look at what we're spending. I'm not tracking every purchase. But I need to see where things are going, or I get nervous.

I think the anxiety isn't really about the amount of money we have. It's that I'm not earning anything anymore. Money just leaves now. Every month, it goes out, and nothing comes back in. After working for 45 years, it just feels wrong.

The Relationship Renaissance

Eight months in, my relationships had reconfigured entirely. Work friendships I thought would last forever evaporated. Family relationships I'd neglected for decades bloomed. New friendships formed from shared interests rather than professional proximity.

Ed and I reconnected. Without work stress and competing schedules, we remembered why we married. We started dating again—actual dates, not just eating dinner in front of the TV.

But it took work—conscious, intentional relationship building. Retirement doesn't automatically improve relationships. It reveals them. And what's revealed requires attention, sometimes professional help, always patience.

Taking Care of Yourself

Eight months in, my body finally adjusted to life without workplace stress. The chronic issues, insomnia, back pain, and digestive problems have mostly been resolved. But retirement brought new challenges. Without my daily walk from the parking lot and around the office, I gained 8 pounds in three months. The mental fog that set in around Month Two was almost as concerning.

Staying healthy in retirement takes actual effort.

I walk every morning now. Not because I love exercise, I don't. But if I don't walk, my brain feels foggy by lunchtime.

We bought a treadmill in 2018. It sat there gathering dust the whole time I was working. Now, when it's too cold or rainy, I use it. Most days anyway.

The physical stuff is only part of it, though. Your mental health can go downhill fast. The isolation sneaks up on you. One day you're fine, the next week you realize you haven't talked to anyone in days, and you feel terrible.

I'm not trying to be perfectly healthy. I'm just trying to build habits that keep me functional. That let me do what I want.

The Unexpected Joy

Last Tuesday, I was sitting on my porch drinking my second cup of coffee around 10 in the morning. And I realized I felt... good. Really good. Not pretending and not trying to convince myself. I just felt okay. Happy, even.

Over what? Nothing big. I read an entire book the previous day. Went to the grocery store at 10 AM when nobody else was there. A friend called and asked if I wanted lunch, and I said yes without checking my calendar. I wore the same sweatshirt three days in a row. Nobody cared.

I couldn't tell you what day of the week it was half the time. And that was fine.

When someone wanted to talk, I could listen. Not just sit there thinking about what meeting I had next. Just listen.

That's when I knew things were getting better, when I stopped waiting for it to feel good and it just... did.

What Comes After Day 90

So, you made it through the first 90 days. Good. That matters.

You've probably started some routines. Maybe you're not waking up every morning wondering what you're supposed to do all day. The identity crisis isn't quite as sharp. You're figuring it out.

Day 91, though? I need to be honest with you about something. It's not the finish line.

Those first 90 days—that's survival mode. You're just trying not to fall apart. And if you made it through without completely losing it, you did the work.

But there's a difference between surviving and actually thriving in retirement.

I'm at month 8 now. And what I've learned is that around month 6 or so, different questions start showing up. Harder ones. Like: I made it through the transition, but is this really it? Just... this? What am I doing with all this time that matters? Why do I still stay awake at 3 AM worrying about money when our financial advisor keeps telling us we're fine? Why am I hiding in my craft room instead of spending time with Ed?

Those questions don't have quick answers. You can't toolkit your way through them in a weekend. They need different work. Deeper work.

Which is why I'm working on a second book right now. It covers months 3-24—the phase I'm in. I'm not writing it because I figured everything out. I'm writing it because I'm in the middle of figuring it out, and maybe what I'm learning can help you too.

The second book gets into what comes after you stop drowning. Identity work that goes past "I'm not my job title anymore." What to do with financial anxiety that won't quit, even when you've done the math. How relationships keep shifting and what to do about that. Finding purpose when it's quieter and different from the kind you had at work. Actually, taking care of your health instead of just talking about it. Making all these systems work when they're pulling you in different directions and planning for what comes after year 2.

I'm eight months in. Still building this. Still getting it wrong sometimes. Still wondering if I'm doing retirement right or if there even is a "right." But if you want to keep going with this—if you need more than just survival strategies—I'll keep showing up.

Right now, though, take a minute and recognize you made it through 90 days. That's real. You got through something hard.

The next phase is different work. But you have already proved you can do hard things. When you're ready, the rest is there.

Thank You

Thank you for reading this book.

When I started this journey—navigating my own unexpected retirement and then sitting down to write about it—I never imagined how much it would mean to connect with readers like you. You could have chosen any number of books about retirement, but you picked mine. That means more to me than I can say.

If this book helped you in any way, would you consider leaving a review? It doesn't have to be long or elaborate. Even a few sentences about what you found useful would help other people decide if this is the right book for them. And your honest feedback—what worked, what didn't—helps me write better books.

I'm not a financial planner or a celebrity guru. I'm just someone who's been where you are—or where you might be headed—and I want to help make this transition a little easier for others. Your voice matters in that mission.

Thank you again for letting me be part of your retirement journey.

With appreciation,
Cheryl

A Final Word on the Research Behind This Book

Throughout this book, I've included research and statistics to back up what I experienced.

This is my story. What happened to me. But I wanted to show you it wasn't just me being weird or failing at retirement. Other people go through this, too. There's actual research on it.

The numbers and studies I mention? They're real—peer-reviewed research, surveys from actual institutions. I'm not just making claims and hoping you believe me.

I didn't cite every study I read. There's a lot out there. I selected the ones that made sense, seemed solid, and supported what I was trying to say. If you want to read more about any of it, you can look up the studies I mentioned. Most of those institutions have additional resources that might help you if you're dealing with these challenges yourself.

The bottom line? What you're experiencing is real. It's documented. And most importantly, it's survivable.

Bibliography

AARP. *Life After Work Survey.* AARP Research, 2022.
https://www.aarp.org

American Psychological Association. *Identity and Well-Being in Career Transitions. Journal of Career Development Review*, 2022.
https://www.apa.org

Boston College Center for Retirement Research. *Involuntary Retirement Adjustment Study.* CRR, 2021.
https://crr.bc.edu

European Centre for Social Welfare Studies. *Social Networks in Retirement Report.* ECSWS, 2022.
https://ecsws-eu.org

European Social Science & Aging Survey. *Social Connection & Aging Report.* ESSA, 2023.
https://essa-eu.org

Gallup. *Well-Being in Retirement Survey.* Gallup Research, 2023.
https://www.gallup.com

Gerontological Society of America. *Aging Solo Study. The Journals of Gerontology*, 2023.
https://academic.oup.com/gerontologist

Harvard Medical School, Study of Adult Development. *Insights from Eight Decades of Life Course Research.* Harvard University, 2023.
https://news.harvard.edu/gazette/story/2023/01/harvard-study-what-makes-us-happy

Journal of Gerontology. *Stress & Role Transitions Study.* 2022.
https://academic.oup.com/gerontology

King's College London. *Cognitive Adjustment in Early Retirement.* Institute of Psychiatry, 2023.
https://www.kcl.ac.uk

MassMutual. *Retirement Happiness Study.* MassMutual Research, 2024.
https://www.massmutual.com

Mayo Clinic. *Healthy Aging & Daily Rhythm Report.* Mayo Clinic Healthy Aging Program, 2022.
https://www.mayoclinic.org

Mental Health America. *Depression in Older Adults: Prevalence and Care Gaps.* MHA, 2023.
https://mhanational.org

National Academy of Sciences. *Social Isolation and Health Outcomes in Older Adults.* NAS Press, 2020.
https://www.nationalacademies.org

National Bureau of Economic Research. *Time Use and Well-Being in Retirement.* NBER Working Paper, 2021.
https://www.nber.org

National Institute on Aging. *Healthy Transitions Study.* NIA, 2022.
https://www.nia.nih.gov

Stanford Center on Longevity. *Purpose & Daily Meaning Study.* Stanford University, 2022.
https://longevity.stanford.edu

Stanford Center on Longevity. *Retirement Transition Study.* Stanford University, 2023.
https://longevity.stanford.edu/retirement-transition-study

Stanford University, Social Well-Being Project. *Social Roles & Aging Study.* Stanford, 2021.
https://wellbeing.stanford.edu

Transamerica Institute. *Retirement Transitions Report.* Transamerica Center for Retirement Studies, 2023.
https://www.transamericainstitute.org

University of California San Diego. *Purpose & Aging Study.* UCSD Center for Healthy Aging, 2022.
https://healthyaging.ucsd.edu

University of Chicago. *Later-Life Purpose & Engagement Study.* Center for Aging and Human Development, 2022.
https://aging.uchicago.edu

University of Exeter. *Later-Life Competence & Engagement Study.* Center for Aging Research, 2023.
https://www.exeter.ac.uk

University of Michigan. *Health and Retirement Study: Social Dynamics Report.* Institute for Social Research, 2021.
https://hrs.isr.umich.edu

University of Toronto. *Retirement Adjustment Study.* Department of Psychology, 2023.
https://www.utoronto.ca

Urban Institute. *Early Retirement Adjustment Report.* Urban Institute, 2020.
https://www.urban.org

The Retirement Journey Series

Thank you for reading *The Hidden Side of Retirement*. I know how unsettling this transition can feel, especially when it looks nothing like what you expected. If this book helped you feel a little more grounded and a little less alone, then it has done what I hoped it would do.

This book is the first in *The Retirement Journey Series*, a collection designed to walk with you through the different stages of retirement, one step at a time. While each book stands on its own, together they are meant to support you as you move from simply getting through the transition to building a life that feels meaningful again.

To support you further, I invite you to visit my website, where you can download the companion Toolkit PDF referenced throughout the book. The toolkit includes assessments, exercises, and practical resources to help you reflect, evaluate your readiness, and apply what you have read in a way that fits your life. You will also find updates on future books in *The Retirement Journey Series*, along with additional insights and resources as they become available.

Retirement is not a single event. It is a process. You do not have to have it all figured out at once, and you do not have to navigate it alone. I am honored to be part of your journey and to continue learning alongside you as we each explore what comes next.

With gratitude,
Cheryl Fimbel

Connect with Cheryl at:
Website – CrownYearsMedia.com
Email – Cheryl@CrownYearsMedia.com
Facebook – BetterLifeOverFifty
Instagram – @chfimbel
LinkedIn – Cheryl Fimbel
YouTube – @BetterLifeOverFifty

About the Author

 Cheryl Fimbel understands the emotional upheaval of retirement firsthand. After a 45-year career in healthcare leadership, guiding organizations through major transitions and regulatory change, she now brings that same change-management expertise to helping individuals navigate the psychological challenges of retirement.

Cheryl's career began with dual undergraduate degrees in Business Management and Accounting, followed by more than two decades as Director of Accounting and Information Systems at a 300-bed hospital. She later spent 13 years leading ambulatory health systems implementations for a major Houston health system and went on to serve as Director of Quality Informatics for a national physician group. Throughout her career, she specialized in leading teams through complex system implementations and organizational disruption, an experience that deeply informs her approach to retirement transition.

As the primary provider for her family, Cheryl's position was unexpectedly eliminated just one year before her planned retirement, only weeks after her mother's death. The anxiety, loss of structure, and identity questions that followed became the foundation for her work addressing the emotional side of retirement that financial planning often overlooks.

Drawing on research, data-driven tools, and personal experience, Cheryl developed the assessments and exercises featured in her retirement toolkits. She writes with the warmth of a thoughtful conversation, addressing the real questions retirees face as they redefine purpose and routine.

Cheryl lives in North Texas with her husband, Ed, stays closely connected to her family, and continues exploring what it means not just to survive retirement, but to build a life that feels genuinely meaningful—one day at a time.